As We Are Now

A NOVEL BY

MAY SARTON

W · W · NORTON & COMPANY · INC · *New York*

Copyright © 1973 by May Sarton

FIRST EDITION

Library of Congress Cataloging in Publication Data

Sarton, May, 1912–
  As we are now.

  I. Title.
PZ3.S249As3   813′.5′2   73–7555
  ISBN 0–393–08372–1

Published simultaneously in Canada
by George J. McLeod Limited, Toronto
PRINTED IN THE UNITED STATES OF AMERICA

1 2 3 4 5 6 7 8 9 0

As you are now, so once was I;
Prepare for death and follow me.

New England tombstone

As We Are Now

I am not mad, only old. I make this statement to give me courage. To give you an idea what I mean by courage, suffice it to say that it has taken two weeks for me to obtain this notebook and a pen. I am in a concentration camp for the old, a place where people dump their parents or relatives exactly as though it were an ash can.

My brother, John, brought me here two weeks ago. Of course I knew from the beginning that living with him would never work. I had to close my own house after the heart attack (the stairs were too much for me). John is four years older than I am and married a much younger woman after Elizabeth, his first wife, died. Ginny never liked me. I make her feel inferior and I cannot help it. John is a reader and always has been. So am I. John is interested in politics. So am I. Ginny's only interests appear to be malicious gossip, bridge, and trying out new recipes. Unfortunately she is not a born cook. I find the above paragraph extremely boring and it has been a very great effort to set it down. No one wants to look hard at disagreeable things. I am not alone in that.

I am forcing myself to get everything clear in my mind by writing it down so I know where I am at. There is no reality now except what I can sustain inside me. My memory is failing. I have to hang on to every scrap of information I have to keep my sanity, and it is for that purpose that I am keeping a journal. Then if I forget things later, I can always go back and read them here.

I call it *The Book of the Dead*. By the time I finish it I shall be dead. I want to be ready, to have gathered everything together and sorted it out, as if I were preparing for a great final journey. I intend to make myself whole here in this Hell. It is the thing that is set before me to do. So, in a way, this path inward and back into the past is like a map, the map of my world. If I can draw it accurately, I shall know where I am.

I do not blame John. That is the first thing. In his way he is fighting to keep whole, as I am, and Ginny was making life intolerable for both of us. Far better to dump me here than lose me in a quicksand of jealousy and hatred. He had to make a choice. The only thing I do not know is why he has not come to see me. Perhaps he is ill. Perhaps they have gone away. It does seem queer.

Also, although it is clear in my mind that I had to go somewhere, it is not clear why the place chosen should seem a place of punishment. But I must not dwell on this if possible. Sometimes old people imagine that everyone is against them. They have delusions of persecution. I must not fall into that trap.

It is better to smile at the image of that big white Cadillac turning off macadam onto a rough dirt road, the rain —of course it had to be raining, and not just a quiet rain, but a real downpour that would make almost anyone consider building an ark! I wondered whether Ginny had taken a wrong turning. When we stopped at a small red farmhouse that looked as though it had been gradually sinking into the mud for years, I thought it must be to ask directions. There was no sign, only two elms—the nursing home is called "Twin Elms." Five enormous geese stretched out their necks and hissed at us when we got out of the car. I noticed there was a barn over to the right. In the rain, the whole place seemed enclosed in darkness.

"Well," John said, "here we are, Caro." His voice had become unnaturally cheerful in the way voices do when addressing children or the feeble-minded.

There were two doors, but the front door opened into a sea of mud and was evidently not used. Ginny had parked close to the side door. We pushed our way in without ringing because of the downpour. Even in those few minutes I got soaking wet. There was no hall. We found ourselves in a large room with four or five beds in it. There was no light on. It took a moment before I realized that beside each bed an old man sat on a straight chair. One had his head in his hands. A younger man, whose legs were bandaged and who was half lying and

half sitting in a sort of medical rocker, tried to speak but
half choked. He was clearly out of his mind. However, he
smiled, the only person in that room who did or who
could.

Ginny called out loudly, "Here we are! Is there anyone
home?"

Then an enormous woman filled the doorway, wiping
her hands on her apron.

"Oh . . . well," she said, as if she had been taken by
surprise. "My daughter is just making up Miss Spencer's
room. But I guess you can go in now." She laughed.
"We're up tight these days, no place to ask you to sit
down."

I had had so many shocks by then that I felt quite
numb and only wanted to be left alone as soon as possi-
ble. My heart started up and I was afraid I might faint.
But it was a comfort to find that I had a room of my own,
just big enough for a bed, an armchair, and a bureau. The
bed was parallel to the window, and the window looked
out, much to my astonishment, on a long field with tall
trees at the end and, beyond them, gentle hills.

"Look at the view," Ginny said. "Isn't it marvelous?"

"What is that woman's name?" I asked in a whisper. I
had the feeling already that even a whisper would be
heard.

"Mrs. Hatfield—Harriet Hatfield. She is a trained
nurse." (That is what Ginny said, but of course she must
have known that Mrs. Hatfield's only experience had
been as an aide in the State Hospital for two years.) "She

and her daughter work very hard to keep things going here."

There was dust under the bureau and an old piece of Kleenex.

John disappeared for a time. They brought me a cup of tea and a cheap biscuit, which I didn't eat. They offered to help me unpack my two suitcases, but I managed to make it clear that I am not infirm. I set the photographs of my mother and father and one of me with John when I was fourteen and he was in college on the bureau, and three things I treasure: a Japanese bronze turtle, a small Swedish glass vase, and the *Oxford Book of English Verse.* I found my little pillow and lay down on the bed then. After a while I recited the Lord's Prayer three times. I do not believe this prayer is heard by the Person to whom it is addressed, but I find it comforting, like a rune, something to hold onto.

When John and Ginny left, he said, "We'll be seeing you."

After a while I slept. The rain drummed on the roof. I felt that for a time I must be absolutely passive, float from moment to moment and from hour to hour, shut out feeling and thought. They were both too dangerous. And I feared the weeping. Lately, since the hospital, I have cried a lot, and that may be one reason John felt I must go. Tears are an offense and make other people not so much suffer as feel attacked and irritable. When the inner world overflows in this way, it forces something entirely private out into the open where it does not belong, not at

[13

my age anyway. Only children are permitted tears, so in a way perhaps my being sent here is a punishment. Oh dear, I must not think about that now. Everything is dangerous that is not passive. I am learning to accept.

Harriet Hatfield woke me, not ungently, and pretty soon her daughter, Rose, came in with my supper on a tray. At least I do not have to eat with the others and watch them spill their soup. I can lie here and look out at the hills. Supper was cornflakes with milk and a banana that first evening. I enjoyed it far more than one of Ginny's "gourmet" concoctions. But then I could not sleep. I had to get accustomed to the noises, queer little creaks, the groans and snores in the big room where the men are. It seemed a terribly long night. When I went to the bathroom I bumped into a chair in the hall and bruised my leg. Perhaps John will bring me a flashlight when he comes. I will ask for note paper and stamps, a daily newspaper, and maybe a bottle of Scotch. It would be a help to have a small drink measured out each evening before supper.

That thought was a comfort when I wrote it several days ago. Now I know that good things like that are not going to happen. Old age, they say, is a gradual giving up. But it is strange when it all happens at once. That is a real test of character, a kind of solitary confinement. Whatever I have now is in my own mind.

Lately I have thought often of Doug, a former student of mine, who was put in solitary for two years by the Russians. When he came back he talked and talked about it and I listened. I thought I was helping him by listening. I never imagined that one day all he told me would be helping me. One thing he did was make a study of spiders, and later of mice. He remembered all the people he had known in school and tried to imagine exactly what had happened to them since, which amounted to making up novels in his head. He did mathematical problems. But he was under forty when this happened to him, and I, Caro Spencer, am over seventy—seventy-six. Time gets muddled up and what I lack, I fear, is the capacity to stick with a routine, to discipline myself—my mind goes wandering off. I see this all around me—when the TV is on, the old men stare at it in a daze. They do not pay attention for more than a few minutes, even to a ball game. I must try to pay attention to something for at least an hour every day. This last remark struck me as humorous and I laughed aloud after I had read it again. What difference does it make what I do or do not do? (No, that is the devil speaking. Do not listen to the devil.)

My first study became the two women who have me in their dominion. I observed them as if they were mice or spiders. It is better to think of them as beings remote from the human, as another species that flourishes on the despair and impotence of the weak. They are both grossly fat. When they make the beds and their enormous breasts jiggle, the old men leer and wink at each other. Harriet has a lover, an intense wizened little man ten years younger than she who smokes horrible cigars in the kitchen and rarely speaks. There are three children, Rose's, who come to play in the yard while she is here— she sleeps somewhere else. They chase the geese and climb trees and it is nice to have them around although they scream and fight a great deal—all girls. I would prefer boys.

Harriet is a dishonest woman so it is hard to pin her down. She puts on a terrific act when relatives come, coos over some old man whom she has treated roughly when changing his diapers a few moments before. She is full of false compassion at all times. "Imagine," I have heard her say, "we take them in, poor things." (We are talked about always as "them," as if we were abandoned animals thrown out of a car.) "Their families bring them here and sometimes never come back at all!" And the relatives look properly shocked and praise her for taking in these waifs and strays. But it is next to impossible for anyone "outside" to bear this atmosphere of decay for long, I have noticed. People come in, full of good cheer, bringing a carton of cigarettes or a magazine, but after about five minutes they begin to fade out, look hunted, have nothing to say after the first few exchanges about the weather and how their father or aunt is feeling. Paralysis sets in and suddenly they are compelled to flee.

I wonder whether a person who has complete power over others does not always become wicked. I try to separate what Harriet has become from what she may have been ten years ago. Her face is now that of a greedy and sullen pig—small blue eyes, a mean little mouth. It is true that both she and Rose are overworked. It seems as though they were always changing beds, washing someone, or bringing in trays. They too are no doubt affected by the atmosphere, tired most of the time, dealing with crotchety old people who are (let's face it) most of them not lovable. I gather that the old men are chiefly on welfare.

It is terrible to have to admit that even here one does not change one's class. I am a snob. I went to college, taught school for forty years, come of gentle people. Most of the others here worked with their hands. Deprived of work, they have no resources at all. Two of the old men play cards for hours at a time. One reads the only newspaper very slowly for most of the morning. I have no peer, no one I can talk to. Harriet and Rose address me always as "Miss Spencer" with heavy irony. I am afraid to admit it even to myself but I feel sure that I was resented from the start as "superior."

The idea is that we are all one big family in a cozy old farmhouse, that this is to be truly a "home." Oh dear me! But we are free to wander about. Sometimes I am invited into the kitchen, the one really nice room in the house, with its good smells of cooking, its warmth and bright colors (red and white checked curtains, a new blue linoleum floor, and a big new stove and frigidaire). I sit for a half hour with the family and am given a cup of tea.

"How are you feeling this morning, dear?" Harriet may

[17

ask, but she never waits to hear my answer. With me she is subservient in a nasty way, never rude, but she has, of course, many ways to humiliate me. Thank Heavens I can wash myself and am not bedridden! My body is still my own, not to be degraded by those coarse, hard hands. For how long? At present I have a bath every day—rarely hot, but at least then I can lock the door and have total privacy for a quarter of an hour. The bath is my confessional. I can weep there and no one will see me.

Otherwise there is a house law that doors must not be closed. The two women are always in and out of every room, and one never knows when they are listening. Sometimes I go in and visit with the only other inmate who has a private room. Standish Flint is a retired farmer, American Gothic face, a noble man, but he is extremely deaf now and rarely gets out of bed. Since I have to shout to be heard, we converse more with signs and smiles, with ironic smiles, and sudden guffaws on his part. He whispers, "I never thought it would end like this," then looks hunted for fear "they" will be listening. I understand from Harriet that his wife is living but seriously ill, bedridden, being taken care of by a daughter. So that explains why no one comes to visit him—no one, anyway, in the two weeks I have been here.

Like me he cannot be beaten down yet. He is still his own man. So he is tortured in mean little ways—made to wait too long for the bedpan. Very often he refuses to eat what they bring him (he is on a dull diet of soft foods) and turns his head away. I sometimes think he is trying to starve himself to death. Every one of us still in his right mind must have fantasies of escape, and death is the only practical one. I have indulged in these fantasies myself—but I am still waiting for what will happen next. I want to see my brother. (He can't stay away forever.) There are things I have to do inside myself before I can die. And I have the belief that we make our deaths, that we ripen toward death, and only when the fruit is ripe may it drop. I still believe in life as a process and would not wish to end the process by an unnatural means. Old-fashioned of me, I suppose. Then I suspect that suicide is a kind of murder, an act of rage. I want to keep my soul from that sort of corroding impurity. My soul? What do I mean when I use that word?

Something deep down, true, detached from impurities, the instrument we have been given for making distinctions between right and wrong, true and false—the intrinsic *being* that is still alive even when memory goes. I treasure my soul as something given into my keeping, something that I must keep intact—more, keep in a state of growth and awareness whatever the odds. For whom? For what? That is the mystery. Only when we can conceive of it as belonging to some larger unity, some communion that includes stars and frogs and trees, does it seem valid to "treasure" it at all. I sometimes feel I am melting into the lovely landscape outside my window. Am floated. For an hour I do nothing else but rest in it. Afterwards I feel nourished. I am one with those gentle old hills.

Did they always hate me, my family I mean, because I was different, because I never married, because I didn't play bridge and went off to Europe alone every summer? A high-school teacher in a small town is (or was in the years when I taught math) not exactly suspect, but set apart. Only in the very last years when I was established as a dear old eccentric did I ever dare have a drink in public! And even among my colleagues, mostly good simple-minded fellows, I did not quite fit in. They had their own club and went off fishing together and on an occasional spree to New York, but of course they didn't want an old maid tagging along and their pleasures would hardly have been mine. I can go almost crazy with joy in a museum. I can get drunk on Vermeer or Brueghel, but the average nightclub is sheer misery to me because of the noise. My most intense pleasures were always reading, listening to records, and learning poetry by heart. That has come in handy here, as I sometimes spend two hours saying poems to myself.

"Talking to yourself again?" Harriet sneers when she comes in with my lunch. Why bother to answer? I am too old to try to make connections with boors and sadists.

I can still make connections with an animal and it must be said for this infernal place that it is in no way an "institution," and if it is dirty, at least there are a few animals around. There is a very old collie who wags her tail at the sound of a footstep and likes to be stroked around her ears. She licks my hand when I caress her. And, best of all, there is a cat called Pansy, a black cat with very soft fur, maybe a little coon in her. She has round golden eyes. I have been told categorically that she must not get up on the bed. But occasionally she manages to sneak in late at night and climb up, first curling into a tight ball, then later, when I stroke her, uncurling to lie full length, upside down, sometimes with one paw over her nose. It is hard to express the joy it gives me to stroke this little creature and to feel the purrs begin in her throat. Those nights I sleep well, a lively sleep rather than a deathly sleep. It makes all the difference!

Everybody here is waiting . . . all the time. Standish has been demanding to see the doctor for days now, and I hear Harriet trying to get through. But I guess all the doctors around here are terribly busy, and it's a long way to come. Standish tells me he is in pain—kidneys, he says. He looks white and drawn.

Most of the old men are on tranquilizers, I have discovered—that explains why they are so dull and passive. Only the feeble-minded man, who is quite dear in his own strange way, is eager to talk and smiles when I go in there, but it is next to impossible to understand him. His speech is a sort of gurgle. I cannot imagine why his legs are bandaged all the time. He waits for his father to come; the old men wait for married daughters or sons. I wait for John.

I think it is almost three weeks since they left me here. I get frightened of losing all sense of time. I can't remem-

ber when it was I did come—some time in June, I guess.
It has been too damp or too buggy for me to sit outdoors.
But I could insist on going out at least for a short walk.
Why don't I? I think it is because after a short time, even
a very few days here, one begins to feel like an animal in
a cage. Even if the door were open, one would not dare
move. It is the sense of being totally abandoned, so at
first one goes way down deep into oneself and stays there
just as a frightened animal does. I have an idea now that
John was *told* to stay away. I have often thought about
those visits to people in jail—a few minutes, a visit long
looked forward to, but bringing with it chiefly wild nos-
talgia or despair. The difference is that it is hope that is
hard to handle. Most prisoners foresee a time when they
will get out. Here we know there is no way out, only
down, little by little, till death do us join with whatever
comes next, if only dust to dust. Hope is one thing of
which we are deprived.

One of my problems is that John, after all, is eighty and
has no very clear sense of time passing. He may honestly
believe that he has left me here only a few days. Or
Ginny may have forced him to go on a trip to her people
in Ohio, or somewhere. I have thought of writing but I
wonder whether the letter would be mailed, and I cringe
at the thought that it might be read and thrown away.
Also, if it did get there, Ginny might do the same.

Lately I have come to see that John and I never really
understood each other. We took each other for granted, I
suppose. But I cannot remember any real talk we ever
had—about ourselves, I mean. We talked for hours about

books and about the state of the world. We had fierce ar-
guments that we enjoyed, but our parents were troubled
by our ferocity. Their philosophy was peace at any price,
and if possible under a Republican administration! The
fight went out of John when he married Ginny. Thank
God I never got married, never gave my body and soul
into the keeping of anyone. Unregenerate I surely am,
but I'm myself alone. There is some dignity in that. And I
guess that is why I have not written—"dumb from human
dignity" as Yeats said, but that was about passionate love.

The other day I was lying on my bed having a rather
good think about Alex, the Englishman I loved, off and
on, for twenty years, married of course, so I saw him only
in the summer for brief weekends, and only twice for
journeys we made together, once to Greece and once to
Italy. Harriet interrupted here, and with her sharp needle
thrust into this reverie.

"What are you dreaming about, Miss Spencer?"

"My lover," I said.

I saw her gesture as Rose came in, pointing to her
head, saying without words "crazy as a loon, of course.
This poor old thing never had a lover—senile." It was
written on her face as clear as clear.

Am I senile, I wonder? The trouble is that old age is
not interesting until one gets there, a foreign country
with an unknown language to the young, and even to the
middle-aged. I wish now that I had found out more about
it. Loss of memory—but some things remain so vivid! In
some ways I am not myself, that is true. In the first days I
tried setting up mathematical problems, but I couldn't

seem to concentrate. It is not so much that, though, as that
I am not interested in the abstract cogitation any longer.
I am interested in me. I am a long way still from the ful-
fillment, the total self-understanding that I long for now.
I remain a mystery to myself. I want to get right down to
the core, make a final perfect equation before I am
through, balance it all up into a tidy *whole*. If I could
think of this place not as the House of the Dead but as
the House of Gathering—the house where I have to come
to terms with everything, sort it all out, accept it all, I
think that might be salvation, a rock on which to stand at
least. It is all quicksand and threat still. I cannot get used
to being here. It feels so makeshift. No paintings on the
wall. Dust under the bureau. I never thought I should be
asked to sleep in muslin sheets, or have to swallow daily
doses of sheer vulgarity and meanness of spirit. If this is
Purgatory it is hard to imagine Paradise as in any way at-
tainable, or only in the imagination as a self-created
place.

I am amazed at how much time I can spend apparently
doing nothing, when in fact I am extremely busy with
this kind of dreaming-awake that sustains me.

I have never liked women very much, too intense. I
have been passionately attracted to one or two in my life,
but that is different from liking. I like men much better.

No woman would bear what Standish does in the way he does—so tart and bitter, so authentic. He is too angry most of the time to be sorry for himself. Anger keeps him alive. It is truly hard that we cannot *talk*. If only he were not so deaf. He looks at me with very bright clear eyes when he is awake and (how absurd this is!) I find that I try to look as well as I can for him. My hair needs washing and a rinse. They promise, but of course these things never do get done. But Standish notices a bright scarf or a piece of jewelry and gives me a wink of approval. I would write him messages, but apparently they have lost his glasses—he says he can't read anymore. But sometimes he talks about his life, how hard it has been, how hard he worked, how finally he realized he would have to give up the farm as he couldn't take care of the herd of cows himself and could not afford help. He had saved ten thousand dollars but it all got eaten up when his wife became ill, or almost all—he *says* he pays for himself here. I do hope it is true. Probably it is or he would not be allowed a room of his own.

What keeps him alive is a deep, buried fire of anger that never goes out, apparently. Out of rage he refuses to eat anything for several days. I feel he is always planning a way to get around "them," a way to get back at "them" by sheer tenacity, by passive resistance. Among the sheeplike herd we two are a different breed, rebels. Standish manages usually to get rid of the tranquilizers, hides them, then gives them to me to throw down the john. "They won't get my head," he whispers to me. "They won't castrate me in that way. I'm still alive from here up," he whispers, his hand at his throat. He has good hands, worn, but thin and sensitive. Sometimes I wish I could take one in mine and hold it hard—"We shall overcome." I don't because he is a touchy old man, and probably his chief escape is sexual fantasy.

He talks about Harriet and Rose as if they were prostitutes, with considerable relish, and expatiates on their enormous bums and breasts. He has a repertoire of dirty jokes—childish jokes they are. I do not mind them and some are even quite funny. He gives a loud guffaw after telling me one, and then a quick look hoping he has shocked me. I suppose he imagines I am an old maid—I could tell him some things but they are not to be shouted. So I let him talk, and when he falls asleep I go back to my room. The conversational opportunities here are certainly at a minimum. But then we all talk to ourselves in a perpetual exercise of free association.

I never thought much of psychiatry, but occasionally I imagine when I am lying here on my bed that I am talking to a wise and omniscient listener, a Doctor of Souls to whom I can say things I might not dare say to myself alone. Next time Harriet asks whom I am talking to, I'll tell her, "My psychiatrist, so you'd better leave us alone." Then she'll be sure I'm crazy. And perhaps that is not a good idea. One could make oneself mad by pretending to be, I have sometimes thought. The borderline between reality and fantasy is so thin in this confined, dreadfully lonely place.

:

I have not been able to write for days. I feel very be-
wildered and undone by John's visit—at last—after *four*
weeks! Of course Ginny stayed with us the whole time. It
was a terrible failure on my part, because as soon as I saw
them I began to cry so terribly that I couldn't speak. I
begged them to take me away. That was my second mis-
take. John sweated it out, I suppose, and Ginny talked a
blue streak. Luckily I had made a short list of absolute
necessities and Ginny promised to see to them and to
come back alone in a few days. The list was stamps, note
paper, lavender cologne, to order me the daily Boston
Globe, to see that mail is forwarded (there must have
been *some* since I left their house, magazines if nothing
else), a summer wrapper, a pair of comfortable shoes, a
raincoat, and several books.

John did kiss me goodbye, but he couldn't offer any
comfort. He gave me a ten-dollar bill to put in my purse.
It was done rather awkwardly, and I did not thank him.
They stayed about fifteen minutes. I witnessed in my own
flesh that we become moral lepers here, untouchables,
from whom relatives flee because they can't bear what
they have done.

"It'll get better, Caro," Ginny kept saying in her bright
sharp voice. "Change is always hard at your age." But I
am *not* ninety, nor am I insane! They brought me a car-
ton of cigarettes. The doctor warned me—they must

know that—that smoking could be fatal after the heart attack. Well, perhaps, the kindest way of offering suicide! I shall ration myself, and see. More likely they simply forgot about the heart because they have shut me out of their minds.

Harriet kept lurking around the corner and just when I tried to tell them about how awful it is, she came in ostentatiously with a cup of tea for me, cooing, "Here, dear, this will make you feel better."

"Nothing will make me feel better," I answered. I had an impulse to knock it out of her hands, but restrained myself. Then she addressed herself to Ginny as if John and I did not exist.

"Miss Spencer has been very good," she said. "Of course she's a lady and we are a bit rough and ready for someone like her, but she never complains, do you, dear? They all go through a period of adjustment, you know, and visits are quite hard on them sometimes."

I was wracked with sobs from sheer rage and despair.

"Here's a Kleenex . . . blow your nose, dear, and you'll feel better."

I couldn't wait for John and Ginny to go. I felt as though I were breaking into pieces with shame and misery. Wanted only to be left alone, and now, damn fool, I am weeping again from writing this down.

How long a journey will it be and what must I do to myself to learn to control my feelings here? Let woe in and it's next to impossible to get it out again. The only person who helps me is Standish. He said, "Come in here, woman, and stop bawling. If I were you I'd say a dirty word. I'd say several. Didn't stay long, did they? Families are great until you really need them. I never asked a living soul for anything, and now look at me! Shit," he said, "shit on the lot of them!"

But I can't curse John. He couldn't even look at me, he was so miserable.

Later I took the tranquilizer Harriet gave me. But I must not do that again. It made me feel very logy and queer. All I have is my mind and I must keep it clear. Remember that, Caro. *Don't let them steal your mind.*

Today is a dismal day, pouring rain and wind. The trees bend and strain, and leaves and twigs are torn off, a chaotic world, even outdoors. I put on my pink blouse to cheer myself up, but it seems to me I look queer and gaunt since I came here—there is already a change in my face, so it startles me each morning. Can this worn-out, haunted old body be me? My eyes used to be so blue but they have faded. And my mouth, rather stern at best, looks thin-lipped; deep lines pull it downward. My neck anyway is pretty good for an old bird—none of those scrawny tendons showing. My pearl choker hides the wrinkles. But time at a mirror is worse than wasted time, Caro. It makes you feel depressed. Better turn the mirror to the wall.

Until lunch I am going to lie here and watch the rain and remember all the picnics Alex and I had together. We used to take sketchbooks and go off in his ramshackle

little car, with a bottle of wine, cheese and bread, pâté
when we were in France, a pear or an orange. We had
our worst arguments sometimes about choosing THE
Place. How ridiculous we were! But it had to be just
right, with both shade and sun if possible—once high up
on a hill in a beech wood, looking down over a field, bril-
liant shining gold with buttercups and marvelous swan-
like clouds going over all that day. For a change it did
not rain. What did we talk about all those hours? Alex
worked at Barclay's Bank, some sort of junior officer—he
never wanted to talk about *that*. But he read everything,
a very wide-awake man with a bold, strong face, bright
blue eyes and a wonderful chuckle when he was amused.
And for some reason I amused him very much, the vio-
lence of my language, my American accent. We met in
the National Gallery, classic encounter, in front of the
Piero della Francesca Nativity. I always did feel that
painting says something of great importance—stark, aloof,
yet so moving because of the spaces. It struck me as a
kind of spiritual equation and I pondered it that day, un-
aware until he spoke of the man standing beside me.
"Rather a jolly thing, what?" I was so taken by surprise,
to be addressed in that extremely quiet place, and to be
addressed by an Englishman out of the blue, and what he
said seemed so ridiculously inadequate that I laughed
aloud.

"What's funny?" he asked, lifting an eyebrow.

"Such a jolly understatement!"

He gave me a keen look then, taking me in, American
written all over me. "What do you see in it?"

From there we talked. He guessed I must be a poet, I guessed he must be a lawyer. We agreed that Piero would appeal to a math teacher. (Oh, I do wish I had a reproduction of the painting here!) Alex asked me very good questions. He really liked women. I decided long ago that American men really don't—and before I knew what was happening we were sitting at Rules eating salmon and drinking hock. It was not an instant love, but it was instant recognition, rather a different thing. We enjoyed each other. I felt cherished and admired in a way I never had been before. That first summer we were not lovers. I was frightened, and also dismayed when I learned that he was married. But we wrote long letters to each other the next winter and when we met the following summer we knew that we had become deeply attached. Forty-five years ago! A love affair was a momentous journey to undertake for a person of my sort. But it helped, of course, that I was far from home. No one at home need ever know. And Alex persuaded me, for my sins, that since his wife had a lover, there was no reason why he shouldn't engage himself in the same way. I got very fond of Sarah . . . life is so much stranger than anyone could believe! As I think back, it seems to me that we all behaved in a rather civilized way. There was no drama, no pulling and tearing. Alex did not want to divorce Sarah and I could see why. In many ways he was dependent on her. And she had an elusive charm, was extremely feminine, chic and capable. He liked comfort, order, and beauty, and all these she provided in an amusing little house in Chelsea with an infinitesimal garden at the back that she made into something as perfect as a scene inside an Easter egg.

Did I want to marry him or did I just screen that possibility out? At one time I hoped to have a child by him—quite mad, of course, and Alex would have been dismayed at the prospect. They had two little boys, away at school when I first met Sarah.

I believe that I wanted exactly what I had—that sense of adventure, those picnics, our zany travels together, the depth and range of our communion, yet without any of the usual responsibilities. I doubt whether I would have made Alex a good wife . . . the very thought of what would have been expected in the way of womanly grace and skill terrifies me even now. I was lucky. Only the goodbyes when I had to leave to go home each autumn were excruciating. I felt each time as though I were being asked to cut off an arm or a leg—an amputee. In those days we traveled by boat, of course, and the journey home was limbo. Often I stayed in bed for three days, tortured by missing him, and missing the part of myself that did not live at all in America. It was hard even to write for the first weeks, as words seemed an inadequate substitute for kisses, for all that touch made happen between us—and I am not one to write love letters. I find them embarrassing. Words, except in poems, were not meant to be used as counters in a sensual game. Alex wrote me poems but they were not very good—dear man.

By letter we exchanged our lives, what we were thinking and doing. As the months of separation wore on they became quite abstract, full of philosophical speculation. Amazing that it lasted nearly twenty years, and died, finally, chiefly because of the long separation through World War II. Alex was in some secret work and couldn't tell me, anymore, anything about his day-to-day life. I sent food packages to Sarah every week, and, strangely enough, she and I wrote more intimately at that time than he and I did—the tides changed, the emotional tides. I would like to write more about this but I am tired. The word "picnic" has taken me on a long journey into the heart land, and in some way has given me peace.

John's visit seems rather irrelevant now. I am over the shock. Perhaps it is better that they do not come again, or very rarely. It just seems so unbelievable that I, Caro Spencer, should find myself here *for good.*

Well, it turned out to be one of the worst days after that small interlude of peaceful memorializing. Our lunch was some sort of luncheon meat again, bread and butter, canned beans, and jello. I asked for mustard and was told there wasn't any, a patent lie. Standish threw his lunch in the waste basket. I felt he had been getting a slow burn these last days and was sure to break out sometime. I guess the lunch was the last straw (Jell-o and bread and butter are the only things on his diet). He shouted obscenities at Rose, who burst into tears. Then Harriet came and told him he was a dirty old man and would have to be forcibly fed. I could hear him yell, "You just try that and you'll be sorry!"

But he is so weak, poor tortured beast, that the anger left him white and exhausted. If only I had a bottle of Scotch: a little drink would have done him good.

The old men in the big room were unsettled by all the shouting, and even the always cheerful feeble-minded Jack had a fit of sobbing, a thing he rarely does. We are so like caged animals that moods spread. Today the mood was violently roused *against* our keepers. Apparently no one ate lunch in the end. I could hear Harriet and Rose muttering as they threw it all into the swill pail. They should really keep a pig.

Finally we all went to sleep, that drugged hopeless sleep that is the only escape at times. When I woke at five it was still raining and pitch dark indoors. I put on my light to read in the *Oxford Book* and Harriet came in in a fury and turned it off!

"We aren't millionaires," she raged. "No lights on in summer before six, do you get that, Miss Spencer?" (Heavy irony in her tone as she said "Miss.")

"What about a candle?" I asked. "Would that be allowed?"

"And burn the place down! Are you crazy?"

I held my peace. But one day I am going to break out and smash things. That is what I most fear—the anger that Standish also feels, as it burns its way, little by little, to where it cannot be controlled. I cannot afford the punishment. I am punished beyond what I can handle now. So, Caro, hold your peace, and endure, I tell myself. Or God tells me.

Today I saw the sun rise, peaceful burst of light across
the misty field. It was a small red globe at first, then it
got larger and the light touched everything in long gentle
rays. I felt flooded with joy, as if some inner darkness had
worked itself out like a poison at last. Perhaps it has been
an inch-by-inch taking hold of myself, keeping anger at
bay. I suppose at its most negative it is just "getting used"
to the limits of my prison. For the first days, the first
three weeks until John finally came, I was sick with fear
and disgust. And, in a strange way, I still had *hope*. It
was when hope left me after that visit that I began the
road back, the road into the central self that no environ-
ment can change or poison. I am *myself* again. I know
that I must expect no help from the outside. This is it.
Here I stand.

And here I see what is to be seen. Today, now that the
deluge is over, there are cows in the field, a great comfort.
I often discussed with Alex in the old days why cows are
so peace-inducing, the way they walk along, munching,
in a slow-moving group, the swing of a tail now and then,
the quiet pleasure of creatures leading their own tranquil
lives, creatures eating. Soon the cows will lie down in the
shade, dear things.

It has been altogether a memorable day as the days go
here. At eleven I had not only a letter but the daily news-
paper (so Ginny has at least attended to that for me) and
it was a treat to read it slowly, every page. I suppose it is

[35

possessive to dislike reading a paper that has passed through several hands, that is slightly crumpled. I only wish there were someone I could discuss an article with now and then. I buzz with ideas, but they die away for lack of anything to hang them on, and because I find it hard to think in an abstract sense for very long at a time. It would be a good thing to regard my mind a little as though it were a body out of training, and to force myself each day to use it, to tone up the muscle, so to speak. Today I read at some length about two automobile accidents; one was the cause of death. Beside the copy about that, there was an interview with an officer back from five years in prison in North Vietnam. He said he had been appalled on his return to see how angry we Americans get at the smallest frustration. As he put it, a man gets into his car, and if it doesn't start on the first or second try, he becomes furiously angry. People held up in traffic for even a short while lose their tempers. Can it be true that everyone is so close to rage all the time that the equivalent of stubbing a toe leads to a tantrum? And how can we handle this state of disequilibrium? For that is what it is. Almost every day one reads about some crazy person who takes a shotgun and shoots several people simply to relieve intolerable pressure. But what has caused the pressure? And why must it be relieved only through murderous violence? Questions, questions I can surely never answer . . .

I have saved writing about my letter till last, and now I am stupidly exhausted. It is a letter from one of my former students, married now and with children in high school and in college. Of course she has no idea what has happened to me. And she is far away in Indiana. Yet it felt like a breath of air sent to a person buried alive. For Susie I *exist*, and have existed all these years, maybe thirty-five years, for I was young when she first came to the school, a freckled child with red hair and immense curiosity, nervous, willful, battling her way through school, always in trouble. It was a happy chance for me that math was the one subject she could handle with grace and style—rare gift among girls at that time. So it turned out that I was able to help her with English, at which she was clumsy and inadequate. I'll always remember the day she chased me out to my car after school, breathless as always, and said, "Look, Miss Spencer! Is it a poem?"

I was so afraid of having to disappoint her. While she scanned my face, I read ten or twelve lines describing a seagull, a poem about freedom, I suppose it was meant to be.

"Yes," I said, "it's a poem."

"Oh boy!" She shouted and jumped up and down with excitement. "Oh, thank you"—and she tore off without waiting for whatever else I might have found to say.

I was touched that she had asked me to read it rather than her English teacher, Miss Flood. Miss Flood was a stickler for grammar and punctuation, but she did not exactly inspire her students. And of course she resented me because I did.

I was a good teacher, as I look back on that self now. The point is that I loved math with a passion. I loved the order, the clarity of it, the absolute in it. And I think my students felt that, for me, something more than mere math was involved, an attitude toward life itself. I liked a straight answer to a straight question, in just the way that I felt the beauty of a perfect equation or, even more, a geometric figure.

"You're mad about math, aren't you?" Susie asked me once.

"Am I? Well, maybe. I suppose I see a certain order in the universe and math is one way of making it visible."

She was twelve or thirteen by then, but I always talked to her as if she were grown up. Her mind was worthy of that treatment. And she has not failed. Even when her children were small she got a job with a law firm as a secretary, then when they were in high school, she went to law school herself. Her husband is a Unitarian minister. She studied law with the idea of helping some of the indigent people he has in his ministry who keep getting rooked by loan companies or dealers who persuade them into things they can't afford. Apparently they live in a border district of their industrial town, the church still supported by "old families" who have moved elsewhere, the church building itself now in a part of the city that is at least half black. I'm proud of Susie.

How am I to answer? Shall I tell her my plight? How could she believe it? What can she do? I shall have to think about this—it will come up again. What is my stance as far as old friends go? Pride enters in. I want Susie to think of me as the vital influence I have been. Teachers should perhaps never let their students into their own problems. It is to lay an unfair burden, a little as if a psychiatrist allowed former patients into his private dilemmas. A teacher cannot become too human or too vulnerable or he ceases to be the rock every young person needs. But Susie is forty now—perhaps more. She is grown up. Am I not to honor that fact with the hard truth? How usable would that hard truth be for her? How devastating? And what is the truth? Perhaps there is none. People disintegrate and have to be "taken care of." Why haven't I had the guts to make an escape, she might well wonder. But it is impossible to describe how isolated we are here. The village is at least five miles away, and there is nothing there, no motel, nothing but a General Store which is the P.O. If I called a taxi—and I have thought of this—and simply left, where would I go? I cannot impose myself for life on some friend from the past. The fact is my friends are scattered and there is really no one in my own town, a hundred miles away, whom I could ask for help. I just about pay my own way here. Are there other better places? Horribly expensive and perhaps, *au fond,* no more agreeable. I am no longer the person Susie needed and perhaps still needs. I am an old woman, fighting for her sanity against the odds.

But before I rest, I am going to rough out a letter. Then I can change it if necessary when I copy it out and send it. It could be, at least, a test of whether anything at all can get through—whether a letter will be mailed or censored or thrown away. If I write I am sure she will answer, *if* she gets my letter.

Sometime in September

Dear Susie,

Your letter was a lifeline and I'm afraid I fasten onto it

as the only helpful thing that has come to me for a month. I am now stowed away in an old people's home. My brother, who is eighty and remarried, has done this and cannot really help himself. After a serious heart attack some months ago, I had to give up the little house you remember and go to them. But it did not, and could not, work. So I am here, more or less denuded of everything that might make life livable. I am losing my memory, but otherwise intact. I believe that I have to take this as some final test of my courage and endurance. I want to meet death fully myself.

What is precious is your writing and remembering what I once was, and still am at times. I need your belief that I can make it to the end—not pity, *faith*. If I were tapping this out to you from a prison cell to a fellow prisoner it could not seem more strange or wonderful to communicate with a real human being. I am proud of you. Please believe in the foxiness of this very old party . . . I mean to outwit "them" in the only possible way, that is by not being brainwashed and by remaining,

Yours very truly,
Caroline Spencer

P.S. I still believe there is some order in the universe: only man seems to stray from it.

The day when I roughed out that letter that never got sent, and probably never will, was some time ago . . . I

do not know how many days have elapsed. I am back in
my own room again, weak and grateful for small favors.
What I had been most afraid would happen, happened
. . . it was because of Standish in pain, his face to the wall
. . . I heard him begging them to get the doctor. And
when Harriet answered finally in that hard, bright, we-
know-better voice, "You're not in pain. You're just stub-
born, throw your medicine away, won't eat. If you're in
pain, it's your own fault—" Well, I went berserk, I guess.
All the frustration and anger and pity seized me like a fit.
I screamed awful things at Harriet. I think I may have
even tried to hit her, but she held me at arm's length.
When she let go, I was blind with rage and tears and
hurled a chair across the room and broke it. "You pigs!
You horrible pigs!" I remember sobbing. Finally Harriet,
Rose, and the woman's lover pinned me down and got me
into a room without windows where I lay in the dark for
several days and nights—I do not know how long—
heavily sedated, I suppose. During that time Ginny came
and left what I had asked for, but was not allowed to see
me—for fear I would talk, I suppose. What a relief for
her! That awful attack of anger tore me open to grief.
Also I think the pills they give me are depressants. I wake
up weeping about 3 A.M. and cannot stop. It is happening
now, I cannot see to write and must lie down.

But I have to pull myself together. I can't let them win,
not yet. So, Caro, you've got to build yourself back from
scratch. I have to think ahead of things I can do. Tomor-
row, perhaps I can copy the letter and get it off to Susie.
Oh dear, I am not strong enough to think of goodness

and gentleness, of belief. They shatter me. I am not worthy, a leper—an old woman without control over herself. When I cried so much in the dark it was a small punished child crying, but that is what I have to battle against—the longing to be forgiven, to be accepted again. When they let me out and brought me back, even Harriet was horribly kind, kind as a master is to a slave who has been tortured and will now, presumably, behave herself. I am still in bed, not allowed to get up, but at least I can see the precious light, and the cows, and Pansy comes to purr on my bed. I did not appreciate how lucky I was to have these comforts before. Now I do. Ginny brought lavender water. I can put it behind my ears as my mother used to do when I was feverish. Ginny brought me a light pink summer bedjacket . . . that was so kind of her. Must I learn that even the wicked *mean* well, at least at times?

I have been a snob about these people, that is true. I have felt myself superior. It was one way of surviving. I have also allowed myself to hate. That is wrong. That is to be inferior as a human being. It takes so long to learn these things. It takes time and suffering, the worst kind of suffering, admitting that one has been wrong, admitting that one has failed, abysmally. All my life anger has been my undoing, and now I must pay for it. And I must begin the serious work of self-making that will conquer it forever.

What I long for with a deep ache inside me is sacred music. I long for the Fauré Requiem, for the Haydn "Mass in Time of War," for some pure celestial music that could lift me above myself, into that sphere where great art lives, beyond what man can be in himself, the intimation of the sacred—what cannot be dirtied or smudged by wickedness or by anger, which no threat can touch.

How can I help Standish now? He welcomed me back from the dark place with tears in his eyes and squeezed my hand—how frail his hand is now! I feared to break it with my clasp. But that amount of human trust did us both good. I am so grateful that, wrapped in dignity, and in pain as he is, he found it in him to do that. It was to thank me for fighting in his behalf, clumsy and bad though my fight turned out to be.

Did the doctor come while I was "away?" I hope so much that perhaps they did get him, but I do not dare ask. I would have to shout to ask Standish and I fear punishment. I do not dare ask Harriet or Rose as it will remind them of my tantrum. Would feeble-minded Jack remember? Would he hear a whisper? Do I dare risk it? The old men sit there like miserable caged owls, but they hear and notice everything.

Sometimes I dream that another woman might be sent. I have never wanted a woman around before, but I feel it would help a lot. The place has the reek of old men and old men's fantasies, sexual of course. I long for a woman with whom to share quite ordinary things, like how I can get my hair washed.

Since my outbreak I feel so unlovable, beyond the pale. And this is childhood again. How many times was I sent to bed without supper because I had a tantrum? And how is it that through all my life I never came to terms with this anger inside me? Yet, Caro, remember that

[43

anger is the wicked side of fire—you had fire and that fire
made you a good teacher and a brave fighter sometimes.
Fire can be purifying. It was purifying when the art
teacher, a homosexual, was threatened with dismissal for
moral turpitude, and I went to the head of the school first
and then to the superintendent and managed to save Bob
—he got his tenure. I withered those two affable and be-
wildered men and it was not by being gentle. So, Caro,
try to think now and then that you are a human being,
full of unregenerate anger and sometimes inhabited by
sacred fire. "Child, you are not all bad!" Who said that?

Or am I thinking of Herbert . . . let me find it in the
Oxford Book . . . Oh, what a comfort to find it again,
The Collar:

> But as I rav'd and grew more fierce and wild
>   At every word,
> Me thought I heard one crying, *Child!*
>   And I reply'd, *My Lord.*

At least when I come to the very nub, to the place
where there is nothing, not even belief in the self, I can
still contemplate purity in Euclid, for instance, and in
dear George Herbert. Now I can sleep. I have reached an
island in the ocean of despair.

I think they want to persuade me that I'm not quite
sane. Every now and then Harriet tells me I have done

something (broken a glass, burnt a hole in my sheet) or said something ("I won't stay here another minute") that I cannot remember *at all*. There are also things I *have* done—or believe I have done—like copying out the letter to Susie, that I may not have done. Losing one's memory is terribly disorienting. The danger is to lose track altogether and begin to be whirled about on time like a leaf in the eddy of a brook—then you begin to wonder what is real and what is not, and where you are, and how long you have been there. And finally it is frightening because I can see that what happens next is a growing distrust of everyone and everything. How can I tell truth from falsehood if I can't remember anything?

Well, Caro, you do remember that you write things down in this notebook. Today, as a "temporary stay against confusion," I read it all. Here I have been for at least a month, maybe two—the leaves are beginning to turn. One swamp maple far down the field is scarlet already. Here I have been all that time and I see that this experience is real and that quite a lot has happened. And I am still able to experience it in all its agony and truth. That is something. The old men in the other room have given up or have become totally passive. They are covered over by time like weeds in water, swaying as the currents move, agitated by a change in the atmosphere, but so remote that it is as if they had ceased to live except deep down inside themselves—and what goes on there? A long daydream where food and sex loom large? In an abstract way, hardly real, or attached to reality—it is not a wife they remember but the titillation of watching Harriet's breasts waggle as she stoops, or Rose's immense bum. Ice cream brings a clatter of spoons and toothless smiles. They watch TV with the expressions of cattle, in a stupor, mesmerized but untouched. Is that the way it goes, the way it must go with me? As I re-read what I have written I see that I must make a constant effort to keep as alert as possible, not to let go even about small things—my appearance, for one.

I am keeping the tranquilizers concealed in the bottom of a box of Kleenex. I feel much more alert since I decided not to take them. And I still have that ten dollars John gave me. Someday I can pay someone to make a phone call *outside,* if someone ever comes whom I could ask. I could even get a taxi up here and escape! But if so, where to? No, Caro, there is no escape here. Don't begin to hope again. That is too dangerous.

I'll smoke a cigarette and take a rest from this writing. It is an effort to do it, yet it is also a satisfaction. Because it *is* written down and can be re-read, it is far more substantive than my idle thoughts, or even my most intense thoughts for that matter. It is *outside* me and because I can see it and read it *outside* my mind, I know that I exist and am still sane.

Today I shall ask whether I can go and sit outside. There are chairs out by the barn, fresh air, and the idiotic geese to watch dawdling about, and the leaves turning. Yesterday I was allowed to get up. I even had a cup of coffee in the kitchen. So maybe . . . if I am meek and cheerful about it. No tears, Caro, no abject pleas.

I did get out and it was wonderful. Just being outside this house was a breath of something like freedom. The sun was warm, so warm I took my sweater off. I took note paper with me and the daily paper and pretended I was an ordinary person on a vacation. I saw a cedar waxwing, several robins, and heard a song sparrow. My hearing appears to be intact and my eyes (as long as I have on my glasses) do pretty well still. It was all such a change that I didn't read or write after all. I became entranced by the slight motion in the maple leaves as a light breeze touched them alive. I understood why Hopkins spent hours making drawings of small waterfalls and eddies in a brook. It is the same pleasure, the changes within a pattern as it is affected by a current or by motion in the air. Then when I looked down, the geese made me laugh with their ridiculous antics, their towering necks and hisses when a car drove up, their absurd waddly walk, so full of dignity. The jar leads them and his three wives follow with a young goose bringing up the rear.

"Do the geese have names?" I asked Harriet when I went back in at lunchtime.

"Only a goose would name a goose," she answered in her flat way.

"Well, someone named *me!*" It was an attempt at humor, but one might as well tell a joke to a pig.

She is tired and cross these days. There are rumors that she and the lover will go away for a month to Florida. The telephone is in the hall outside my room and I have heard her trying to get someone to take her place, not easy.

Will it be better or worse if they do go? Of course it depends on the substitute. Certainly it is a gamble as it is possible that we could do worse. On the other hand we might get a retired RN and then Standish would have the care he needs so badly. He has bed sores, I hear. He groans and curses a great deal now and sometimes does not appear to know who I am. He peers at me with a troubled look, trying to remember. I hold his hand, often ice cold, but he does not squeeze it hard as he did when I came out from the dark. He is past feeling that much any more. How long will he hold out? Will no one ever come to see him? I try not to think about him and that is cowardly.

How angry I was years ago when people refused to admit that the concentration camps existed! Then, when the evidence was there—those frightful photographs of piles of emaciated corpses, and the survivors nothing but bones and eyes—people said to me, "Why dwell on it?" I felt that if we turned away by an inch from experiencing the truth as far as it could be imagined, all these despairing people would have died for nothing, their agony itself denied them. The only thing we could do was to *know*. And after the first shock, and the horror that human beings had done this to other human beings, we had to face that, in some depth beyond the rational, we each

have a murderer and a torturer in us, that we are mem-
bers of each other. All my scientific ideas about progress
went down the drain. It was a crisis of faith in man for
any thinking person and, for some, a crisis of faith in
God.

But almost all of us shut ourselves away from what is
painful. Only our own pain brings us back into compas-
sion. My father, a generous-hearted but rather limited
man, imaginatively speaking, touched me when he had
his first operation at over sixty. One day when I went in
to see him, he was, much to my dismay, crying. I had
never seen him weep. "What is it, father?" I asked, and
could not have been more surprised by his answer. "The
concentration camps," he said. "I have been lying here
thinking about those wretched prisoners." Of course he
was sublimating his own misery.

There is a connection between any place where human
beings are helpless, through illness or old age, and a
prison. It is not only the heroic helplessness of the in-
mates, but also what complete control does to the nurses,
guards, or whatever. I wish I could have seen Harriet and
Rose as they were before they opened this ash heap for
the moribund. It may well be that they began not only
with the idea that a nursing home is a sure-fire invest-
ment but with the thought that they would enjoy taking
care of the old whom families abandon for one reason or
another. Rose, so buried in her flesh, sometimes looks out
with an innocent and childlike air, asks something like a
human question. The other day she picked up my lapis
lazuli pin (Alex found it for me at Cameo Corner in

[49

Bloomsbury) and turned it over in her hands with real appreciation of its beauty. (That intense blue, who has ever seen its like?). She said, "Someone who loved you must have given you this."

I was quite taken aback. "Yes—someone who loved me," I answered. Idiotic to have started to weep.

"But Miss Spencer," she said gently, "that is not something to cry about. Let me fix your pillows and straighten things out here a little. The Reverend Thornhill is coming to pay us a visit."

A visitor? I felt wildly excited at the prospect but I was not about to play into *their* hands about this, so I pretended not to care one way or the other.

"And who is this gentleman?"

"Oh, he's the minister at the Methodist Church."

"No doubt it will be edifying."

(Oh dear, that was a mistake. The irony in my tone, unmistakable, and the use of a word beyond Rose's vocabulary, insulting to her. The moment of something like communication was shattered and she went about her business, banging the broom on the bureau, her heavy hands battering everything about.)

The news of an imminent visitor has thrown me off—I have lost the thread of what I meant to consider this morning. Oh yes, about what happens to people who have complete power over others. This would be a far kinder and better place altogether if anyone concerned with us took the trouble to look around, to *sense* things, to observe, and to keep an outsider's eye on our keepers. But initiative of this sort does not appear to exist—there

50]

is a fundamental shyness about interfering. After all, the
daughters and sons of the poor old men here may think,
it is none of our business, and Dad is losing his mind, so
how can we believe what he says? They are told, no
doubt, by social workers and perhaps even by doctors,
scarce as they seem to be around here, that old people
become "mental," a word that has always amused me, as
it seems to suggest the opposite of what it means. They
are told, I suppose, that old people are naturally de-
pressed and that their depression is "built in," and that
the way to handle it is with drugs, not with imagination
or with kindness. And most of them are simple people,
terrified of the very atmosphere of a hospital or a "home,"
ill at ease, not able to be themselves. Harriet's manner
with them is conspiratorial. They talk in whispers to each
other and in falsely jovial tones to the patients, and the
son or daughter leaves feeling that he has done all he can
by paying a visit. The rest is up to the "institution." They
are not people who have ever had the courage to put up
a fight. The police, their bosses if they are factory work-
ers, the "company," the "government" are all terrifying
powers they cannot control or even understand.

Harriet and Rose are really kind to only one person
here, the feeble-minded Jack. He gets little treats. They
make an effort to understand what he says and what he
wants. More than once he has called them to help one of
the old men. He is the pet, an easily distractable but
sweet nature. Possibly it is his total helplessness that has
endeared him, and the fact that he can do no harm, can
never talk "against" them. He is visited by his very old fa-

ther every week. (I presume he was brought here when his mother died.) They sit beside each other, almost silent after the father has said the same thing several times: "Well, my boy, you seem to be in good spirits." The father brings him hard candies to suck. The father is the only visitor I see who does not seem anxious to get away, who seems actually to enjoy seeing his boy. And he always thanks Harriet for taking such good care of "my boy," gives the rocker where Jack is permanently tied in a gentle rock or two, and tiptoes out to the taxi waiting for him in the yard.

I wonder whether homes like this are ever inspected? The deterioration in cleanliness is marked these days—I suffer from the smell of urine. Bedpans are not properly cleaned and are often left around not emptied for hours. Surely there are laws about homes like this? Is it so remote that the powers that be have never got around to inspecting? Or does Harriet (who worked in the State Hospital) have pull that makes her feel safe? Perhaps I can ask a question like this of Rev. what's-his-name if and when he comes—but I must be terribly careful. Impossible to have any privacy. All the doors are open, and Harriet and Rose *lurk* and make sudden appearances if they sense that any criticism is in the air. They will be particularly on the alert where I am concerned because I am articulate and still able to express my feelings. Now, Caro, you've got to *think* this out. Maybe the wisest thing would be to try to impress this Rev. first as a human being, still *compos mentis*, only that. And then, when he comes back—but how long does that mean? In two

52]

months or more? He has never paid a call before. What I
am afraid of, if he is at all sympathetic, is a torrential
overflow of talk. I feel like a person on a desert island who
sees a fellow human being swimming toward him out of
the blue. Try not to hope, Caro. You know it is the most
dangerous emotion now.

Well, Reverend Thornhill came. I had expected a sen-
tentious man in his sixties, I don't really know why—I
suppose because the Methodist minister at home was like
that! How wrong we are to permit ourselves any stereo-
type where human beings are concerned! Richard Thorn-
hill turned out to be a youngish man, a little over forty
maybe. I heard his voice in the next room, a nice warm
voice, "Well, how are you people today? We're in the
great October weather—at least that is a tonic. The drive
up the hill was so splendid!" I heard Harriet making the
introductions and the quiet way he addressed each of the
old men, some of whom mumbled and then were silent,
lapsing into indifference almost at once. I had been so
afraid he would insist on a hymn or at least read the
hundred and first psalm, but he didn't. He was extremely
polite to Harriet and Rose. "It must be very hard," I
heard him say, "but you are doing something greatly
needed." They were quick to explain that it was hard in-
deed, impossible to get help, but they did their best out
of true Christian concern, etc. Standish, in one of his now

rare rowdy moods (no doubt he was stirred up at the idea of a visitor from outside) suddenly shouted "Shit!"

There was a murmur—I couldn't catch the words. Rose ran in to tell Standish to be quiet and not to insult the minister. And Richard Thornhill, bless him, strode right past her and introduced himself.

"Mr. Flint, I'm glad to meet you. May I sit down for a moment?"

"Don't see why not. It's a free country, ain't it?"

"More than he deserves after that dirty word," Harriet sniffed, standing ostentatiously in the doorway. I could see her shadow on the wall, that mountain of flesh.

"Perhaps I could have a little talk with Mr. Flint," Richard Thornhill said gently but firmly.

"Of course. He's been poorly lately, has a lot of pain. And throws his medicine away. What can we do?" She shrugged and went away.

There was a silence. I could imagine that Standish was taking Thornhill's measure, could imagine very well the keen look he gave him. "Are you going to fool me? Are you honest? Who are you?" Then Mr. Thornhill murmured something, but of course Standish didn't get it.

"I'm deaf, God damn it! You'll have to talk louder. Can't hear a word!"

"I would like to help you if I can," poor Richard shouted.

"Help?" The answer shot back. "People in Hell get no help. They just get more Hell." Standish gave one of his bitter guffaws, a kind of curse on the universe. "Yes," he said, "try it, you'll like it." (It was a commercial we had often heard on the TV and it always made Standish laugh. I would hear him saying sardonically to Rose when she brought his supper, "Try it, you'll like it.")

"I know it's not easy, Mr. Flint. It's hard going for you."

"Hard going all my life. That's no news. But just the same. I didn't think it would end like this." Again there was silence. I felt for Richard Thornhill and I admired him for being silent. Sometimes silence is the greatest sign of understanding and of respect. It is far more consoling than words of false comfort.

"Do you have no family?" he asked then, speaking loudly.

"Yes . . . no . . . what does it matter? You talk to Miss Spencer next door, the only person with her wits about her within a radius of ten miles, I guess. She has her hearing. You talk to *her*," Standish said, bearing down hard. "She'll tell you—"

"I will. God bless you."

But this, of course, was a red rag to a bull. "God bless *me?* You're joking! God doesn't have the address. God never got further than the general store in the village. God?" Suddenly he was in one of his rages. "Christ!" he shouted. "I'm an old man. I had a wife, I had children. My wife is dying miles away from me. I'm dying miles away from her. My children?" I could hear the sob wrenched out of him, then: "Talk to Miss Spencer, for Christ's sake."

So that was the introduction. I was lying on my bed in my pink blouse and blue tweed skirt. I had on my best shoes. Richard Thornhill sat down in the armchair beside me and murmured, "I upset him. I didn't mean to."

Harriet, of course, was there in the doorway. But while she said her piece I looked hard at this young man.

"Miss Spencer is our special, Mr. Thornhill. She is sometimes violent, but now she has learned her lesson, we think she is doing rather well. She's such a lady." (So I get back my ironies at their expense.)

I didn't care *what* Harriet said. I had heard it all a thousand times before. I cared about this young man. I liked his face, a little unformed around the mouth, good clear blue eyes, good forehead. He was no fool, and so far he had made no boners. His copybook, as far as I was concerned, was surprisingly clean for a man of the cloth (if that is the locution). In fact, he appeared to be a fairly intact human being and I hadn't seen one for months.

"Yes . . . of course . . . I would like to have a little talk with Miss Spencer." The formula was repeated and forced a retreat, no doubt only a very short distance.

"Perhaps you would have the authority to close the door. As a usual thing it is not permitted." That was my first test of Thornhill and he responded at once by closing the door.

He himself appeared to be relieved no longer to have to try to straddle two opposed worlds. I saw he was troubled and decided to help him out.

"It must be very hard for you to come into a place like this, a place of despair. It is good of you to make the effort."

"Well, Miss Spencer," he said with a smile, "it's part of

my job. I care about human beings or I wouldn't be a minister."

"The problem is that with the old, the senile, there is so very little to be done. I can see that the time you will have spent coming up here to this remote place might well, in your own mind, have been better spent helping some young boy on drugs or some desperate young mother who wants a divorce."

He gave me a rather piercing look.

"I have the care of souls," he said. "I don't believe the soul has an age in human terms."

"Really? That's very interesting. Very few people in this place have any soul. Or it's buried so deep that even you would have difficulty in making contact with it."

"Mr. Flint does," he said firmly. "What can be done for him?"

"Mr. Flint is committing suicide. That means refusing his medicine or managing to get rid of it (I sometimes help by throwing it down the john) and by starving himself. Would you deny him the privilege of dying as fast as he can?"

"You are asking me questions I cannot answer." I saw his face go pale. Poor dear, what has he known of despair?

"I'll try to ask one that can be answered. Has this place been inspected and if not, why not?"

"It's that bad." He was instantly alert. I have observed before that when moral dilemmas are involved, there is nothing more efficacious than something perfectly down to earth and practical. A bowl of soup or a letter to a representative in Congress can work wonders to relieve the conscience.

"I have no point of comparison," I answered. "Perhaps this is better than it seems."

"You are not like the others here. What is your story?" he asked. I felt his strain, his fear of entering a private reserve. And I liked him for daring to ask the question.

"Nothing special." (Be careful, Caro.) "My brother, my only family, is eighty and remarried to a much younger woman. I had a heart attack six months ago—some time ago, my memory fails about such things. I had to give up living alone, and needed care. John tried to make a go of having me live with them. But his wife, Ginny, and I have nothing in common—it couldn't work. We were all three being torn to pieces. And this place was recommended by the hospital. So I am here."

I could sense that he was looking for a formula. What had I been "before"? "You were a professional woman, I presume?"

"A high-school teacher in our home town, a hundred miles from here or more. I taught math. That's all gone now, but I am sustained by poetry and the music I hear in my head."

"You compose?"

"No, but I remember Bach fugues (close to mathematical formulas) and can, so to speak, hear them in my head. Bach and Mozart."

"You have no record player here?"

"No. It is quite expensive—even a place like this is expensive. I can ask for nothing like that."

"No wonder you are sometimes violent!"

"Oh, not about that. I became violent because they wouldn't get a doctor for Standish when he was in great pain. But then I was put in a room without windows for an indefinite time—days anyway. Little by little, Mr. Thornhill, the spirit gets broken here. Maybe it has to get broken. There is no hope and the spirit lives on hope. I am now learning the ways of despair."

"How can I help you? I would like to."

I think that is what he said. I was agitated. I was trying not to weep. I focused on his kind, innocent face, so perturbed and helpless, poor young man. I think I answered, "The worst thing that happens to us here is that we cease to trust. We are lied to about a lot of things—when the doctor will come, what medicines we are taking. The only thing you could do for me would be, I guess, if I could trust you, and even more important, that you did not go away thinking, 'Well, the poor old creature is slightly touched of course, so can I believe her?'"

"You don't seem at all 'touched' to me, Miss Spencer, I assure you."

"I might be by the time you come back." That is the awful thing, that I cannot know how far I have slipped.

"I'll come back soon," he said and got up. "Could I bring some books?"

"That would be marvelous—a good rich juicy long novel, I would be grateful for *that!*"

He shook my hand warmly and we smiled at each other, an open human smile. It is a long time since I have received a present such as that from a stranger. In fact

[59

the whole conversation, short as it was, gave me a tremendous shot in the arm.

For three days after Richard Thornhill's visit I felt better than I have since I got here. I have sat outdoors every morning. Two days ago I woke and looked out and the whole field was silvered over, and that means the leaves are changing fast. It's a blazing world. Going out and sitting in the natural air is a relief from the stifling smells and atmosphere inside. For a little while I forget Standish's misery. For a little while I feel quite alive and myself. The jar comes and eats bread out of my hand. Pansy sometimes appears, a black panther in miniature, threading her way through the long grasses. The sunlight on my hand is a pleasure. I feel warmed somewhere down at that ice at the bone. I take deep breaths, and my heart, that testy animal, beats with a good steady beat.

Yesterday I went for a little walk, but I was scolded when I got back (I guess they feared I might have run away!) and told to tell someone if and when I did such a thing again. My walk was not a success, as I fell on a sharp stone and scraped my knee. This, too, was treated as a misdemeanor, just as it used to be when I was a child. Mother's attitude was that I had somehow been careless or hurt myself to get attention! Probably I think so much about childhood here, not because I am in my second childhood (What a myth that is—children have hope!) but because the humiliations are the same as the humiliations children suffer, like being treated as if they knew nothing or were incapable of adult emotions. I asked Harriet yesterday whether I had ever given her a letter to mail. (I am haunted by whether that letter to Susie ever got mailed.)

"You must be dreaming, dear. You never wrote a letter," she said with her sweet betrayer's smile.

And I am not sure I ever did copy it out, you see. I have the letter as I wrote it and have re-read it several times, but I simply cannot remember copying it or sealing the envelope. I have discovered that one way to remember things is to associate them with an *action*. Years ago an actress told me that it was not hard to remember a part because each line was associated with motion or some physiological event—the body remembers *for* the mind.

I would like now to write a note to dear old Eva, who worked for me for years. I believe she might make the effort to come and see me. The trouble is that my town is fifty miles from where John lives and a hundred miles from here, so it would be an expedition. Her husband would have to drive her and he is terribly busy as he has two jobs, his own farming, and he works on the roads as well. I'm sitting outside now. It is easier to try to reach over the barriers and to wave my hand when I am not a prisoner in my room. So I'll do it now.

What is the date, I wonder? Sometime in September— fifteenth or sixteenth—that's close enough.

September 16th

Dear Eva,

I wish you could manage to pay me a visit here at Twin Elms home . . . I am not sure of the name of the village but you can get it from my brother, John, and directions as to how to get here. It would do me a world of good to see your face. It seems years, though I guess it is only six months since I left home. I am all right. Only it gets lonely.

Sincerely your friend,

Caroline Spencer.

Even if Harriet reads this, surely she will send it. It does not criticize or complain. And I think I have stamps that Ginny sent with some note paper back in my room.

Well, what an adventure! As I was sitting there in the late morning a small car drove up, and out got a pretty girl with a mane of soft reddish hair and very blue eyes, in jeans and some sort of blue sailor shirt, and in sandals. I wondered whose visitor she might be. I had never seen her before and for a moment I had the wild hope she might be a grandchild coming to see Standish. She looked so alive, getting out of the car with a bunch of garden flowers in her hands. She saw me just as the jar saw her and advanced, his neck thrust out, hissing at her.

"Is he dangerous?" she called out to me, half laughing.

He is rather formidable at a first encounter, and her laugh was a little shaky.

"Just showing off before his wives," I called back. "Pay no attention. He's more scared than you are."

(What astonished me was to hear my own voice, as it used to be, quite loud and cheerful for a change! I realized that we speak in whispers indoors. I have not *heard* myself for weeks.)

She ran over to where I was sitting then.

"I'm Lisa Thornhill. My father sent me over because he can't come till next week. You *are* Miss Spencer?" she asked, and when I nodded, "I felt sure it must be you. My mother sent these from our garden—the very end, but she hopes you'll enjoy them."

Impossible to tell the girl how deeply touched I was, not only by the kindness, but the flowers themselves, manna from Heaven.

I sent her in to put them in water, the sun out here would wilt them. When she came back, she went first to the car and picked up three books, two thick English novels (Heaven!) and an anthology of poems I had not seen before. Then she came and sat in the other wicker chair and for a half hour I was in the real human world again. How wonderful that I could see her outdoors, that I did not feel someone was listening. And how wonderful that I was poised, did not weep, and managed to be almost my old self with this charming girl. I did not talk about myself at all. I was eager to hear about her and the whole family.

She is in her last year at high school, the public school

in the town, and will go off to Smith next year. What she likes best in school is biology and, next, photography. The family is one boy and one girl, like mine. But her brother is two years younger than she; entirely absorbed in baseball, she says. He also plays clarinet in the school orchestra. They have been here only two years. Before that her father had a parish in a small town in Connecticut . . . It is tiring to try to remember it all. That is what I shall do before I go to sleep, turn it all over in my mind, fresh food for thought for a change.

But what seems so extraordinary, even miraculous, is that at last I am being sent some help. The only thing I asked Lisa to do was to mail my letter to Eva. She waited while I went indoors for notepaper and copied it out. Harriet, of course, followed me like a bloodhound into my room and asked me what I was doing.

"I'm writing a letter," I said. "Would you like to read it?"

That floored her for the moment. She sniffed and went away to badger poor Standish with more medicine he will try to dispose of, then came back to say, "Too bad to keep that nice girl waiting . . ."

But I have learned to keep silent when curses rise to my lips. I let that pass.

Anyway I got the letter safely into Lisa's hands, a small triumph, but there have been few such lately. It gave me an immense sense of accomplishment, of self-assertion against all the odds here. And Lisa offered to go and fetch Eva if she finds she can't get away otherwise.

"I love exploring the country," she said. "I just got my

license, you see, and it's exciting to drive all by myself. It's mother's car, but she lets me have it." Then she looked at me candidly and asked, "Could I come and take you for a little drive one day?"

I had the queerest reaction to that. It frightened me, I don't know why. I hesitated and she sensed the hesitation.

"I have a bad heart," I said, but it was a lie. It wasn't my heart at all. I think I was afraid that such an expedition would rouse despair.

She was tactful about changing the subject.

"I'd like to come back and talk some more."

"Would you really?" It is beyond my ken to imagine that a charming young girl could *want* to see me, and I suppose there was a challenge in my tone.

"Yes," she said, blushing in a delightful way.

"All right. As long as we have a pact to tell each other the truth. Is that agreed?"

"I thought people always did."

That made me laugh—I'm afraid, a rather harsh laugh. "The truth does not exist in this place. It has become so rare that I can hardly remember what it is to believe what anyone says." But as I saw this hurt her, I added quickly, "I liked your father. It isn't easy to come here and not utter any platitudes or false comfort. I liked him because he was not out to *tell* me anything. He listened."

"And I've done nothing but talk about myself!"

"This time you talked and I wanted to hear. Come again, and I'll bend your ears back!"

"It's a deal," she said, and then it was time to go.

I am writing this in my room. I moved the flowers to the bed table so I could smell the two deep red roses and also the faint bitter smell of chrysanthemums. How starved I am! I realized in the presence of these flowers that every sense except my eyes is starved here—I do have the long field and. the cows and hills to look at. But the smells are so awful that I sometimes hold my nose for a few seconds to be relieved of them. The food is not too bad, but everything is plastic, even the tray cloth (so it never needs to be sent to the laundry), the dishes, and even the glass! And I am very sick of mashed potatoes and colorless meat covered with thick brown gravy out of a can. I cannot even imagine what it would be like to feel a tender caress—my skin is parched like a desert for lack of touch. Of course Pansy, dear Puss, licks my hand and when I stroke her soft thick fur, it is an exquisite pleasure. What I am getting at is that in a place like this where we are deprived of so much already, the small things that delight the senses—food, a soft blanket, a percale sheet and pillow case, a bottle of lavender cologne, a linen handkerchief seem necessities if one is to survive. We are slowly being turned into passive, maltreated animals. I wonder whether memory itself might not be kept alive partly through the *senses*—a mad idea, no doubt. But I know that I felt *physically* refreshed by that lovely girl. And even animals respond to the environment. Pigs, I hear, are not naturally unclean, but so often kept in filthy pens that they *become* dirty and perhaps are more miserable than we know.

These days I take my book into Standish's room and sit
with him. I am not sure whether he is unconscious a lot
of the time or simply too depressed to communicate. He
lies with his hands clasped over the coverlet, a way of
keeping hold of *himself* I think. When he wakes or stirs
he groans. Twice I have imagined that he was actually
dying. Once I ran out to the kitchen and asked Harriet to
come and see. She straightened his pillow, took his pulse,
and then asked me into the kitchen for a "little talk." "It's
a terminal case," she explained, "cancer, and there is
nothing the doctor can do." That, she told me, is why she
has not insisted that he come out. She was quite matter-
of-fact about it all.

"But surely they could help him with drugs for the
pain? Shouldn't he die in a hospital?"

The family have been notified that he can't last much
longer and have promised to come next week.

It is such a lonely death. I feel someone must keep the
vigil, one human being be at his side. So I am there. It is
all I can do. I put lavender on a handkerchief and wipe
his forehead now and then. I was horrified the other day
to see his nails are *black*. But if I complain, they will sim-
ply beat me down. With his eyes closed, as they are al-
most all the time, he looks like a figure on a tomb. I pray
that he may slip away each night, slip away . . . be al-
lowed *out*.

When an infant is born, it would die if no one slapped

its behind and elicited the wail that will help it to take the cruel cold air into its lungs. What rite of passage is there for the dying? I must ask Richard Thornhill about this . . .

Especially where there is no faith in God, what can one do except *be* there, to wipe the cold sweat from a brow or hold a hand (Standish's are ice cold) and try to warm it? I have been in a hospital only once, years ago, for an appendectomy. It was sudden and I had to be put in a room with two other women, one dying of cirrhosis of the liver. There was a curtain between us, but I could not but be present when a very young priest (he couldn't have been more than twenty) came to give her extreme unction. I was moved by his simplicity. When she tried to make a confession, he said, "All that doesn't matter now. God forgives you." How comforting to believe that! But what comfort is there for Standish? Or for me, for that matter? I long for his death for his sake, but when he goes I shall have lost my only friend here. I have needed the illusion that I could still be useful, be needed by someone. The bond between us was very fragile because of his deafness, yet it was *real*. I shall never forget his handclasp when I came out of the dark. We didn't need words. I did defend him in the only way I could. And he knew it.

It's very hard to write today, yet I must. This document is becoming in a very real sense my stay against confusion of mind. When I feel my mind slipping, I go back and rediscover what really happened. It must be true, I wrote it myself. If it were taken away from me I would be in serious trouble. This is my one worst fear. But so far, thank God, Harriet and Rose have not realized that it is dynamite and consider it the maunderings of a senile old woman, like a game of solitaire. I sleep with it under my pillow, and during the day they haven't time to try to read any of it.

Richard Thornhill acted quickly, bless him. But what has happened only shows that we *are* in Hell and anyone who tries to help may make matters worse. Two days after I wrote about Standish dying, state medical inspectors came. I presume they always come without warning and it had been a humdinger of a morning. One old man had a slight stroke; Jack, who is usually cheerful, had a fit of weeping; and Standish (perhaps fortunately) was lucid for the first time in days. The inspectors looked into everything, the unemptied bedpans in the hall, the dirty sheets on Standish's bed. ("We would have to change him every ten or twelve hours and we can't afford that," I heard Harriet say.) They tried to talk to me, but I was careful. After all, they will be gone and I shall be here forever. I was foxy as could be, praised Harriet and Rose, told how hard they worked, and whatever I communicated otherwise was done with a single wink at a crucial question that I answered loudly in the affirmative, "Oh yes, they are very kind here."

The result of this visitation was that Standish was put in an ambulance to be taken to the hospital. "Don't

bother," he implored, "don't take me away!" At the stage
he was at, any move was a threat, his only desire to be
"let be," to die where he lay. He was not permitted that,
and he died in the ambulance among total strangers.

I have to write this very factually, because it is so hard.

His family never came in time. His battle to die with
dignity in his own way was lost. And I was not with him
at the end. This, I feel sure, meant nothing to him, but to
me it has been hard to bear.

Apparently the place is not going to be closed, the
need is too great, and there is nowhere else available to
send us. But I got it from the horse's mouth, Harriet, that
they will no longer be allowed to take people as *physi-
cally* ill as Standish was.

"It's done us only good," she said to me with an air of
triumph. "We won't have to take in the moribund any
longer." Then she gave me a long hard look. "So what-
ever you tried to do, Miss Spencer, has worked only to
our advantage. After this, mind your own business."

"But what have *I* done?" I asked miserably.

"Never mind. *We* know," she said. And I am sure I
shall be punished, but it remains to be seen just how.

Without the Thornhills—Oh, I do hope he comes to see
me soon!—I would feel very much threatened. Reprisals
are inevitable. At present I am ostentatiously ignored, not
asked to the kitchen for coffee, treated like an imbecile.

"Poor Miss Spencer," I heard Harriet say to some visit-
ing relative, "she means well, but she is quite cuckoo. We
have to warn people against anything her deluded mind
makes her invent against us."

To get away from this sordid business, let me think for

a moment, now that I am outdoors and a little more free in my mind, about the *effect* of Standish's death on the other inmates. It took me completely by surprise. Of course they had little or no contact with him in the big room where the old men and Jack are. To them, he was hardly a *person,* as he was to me.

Well, when they heard he had died, there was quite a stir, not of compassion or grief, but of sheer exhilaration that *they*—Roger Thompson who has no teeth, Fred Smith who never speaks, Mr. Coughlin (he is always called Mr., I know not why) who is diabetic and comatose most of the time, and Sam Martin who reads the newspaper line by line—are alive and Standish is dead! The outer room has never been more lively. They got together and demanded ice cream. They had fits of laughter at obscene jokes Fred told. Since I came here they have seemed like the living dead. But apparently they are intoxicated by the thought that someone dies but *they* are still here, more or less alive (far less alive than Standish even when he was dying—his frail hands spoke so poignantly of a *soul!*) They have reached the stage almost of amoebas—open mouths and a digestive tract, what more? Yet life, even that primeval life they still hang onto, means this—triumph when someone else goes under! They have become incapable of pity.

They gave me salt instead of sugar for my coffee this morning. On purpose? I rather think so. I wept with ag-

gravation, but I pretended it had not happened. I am too
vulnerable these days—I have been tossed about on
nights of very little sleep. (How wonderful then when the
sky lightens over the distant trees at last, and the birds
chirp and sing! Reprieve.) Worse than those nights are
the ones when I *do* sleep and have nightmares. In the
middle of one of those I got out of bed and fell, but at
least nothing was broken. I badly bruised one thigh on a
chair. It has a huge purple splotch on it and hurts quite a
lot. At the time it was a relief to wake, even though I
woke in pain on the floor, terribly frightened. I thought I
was on a ship, running down horrible white corridors to
try to get to air, but always I came to a locked door. I
find it impossible to read. I just can't pay attention.
Whatever it is going on inside me, like troubled ocean,
gets in the way. Sometimes, lying here on my bed, I feel I
am drowning.

"What's the matter with you?" Rose asked when she
came in yesterday while I was having one of these spells.
She felt my forehead. It was clammy with sweat and my
hair soaked through. "Let me bring you a hot water bot-
tle," she said quite kindly. And she actually did so. (I
have an idea that Harriet, who certainly has it in for me
since the inspectors came, was outside or had gone out.)

"There now," Rose said as she slipped the hot water
bottle in under the covers, "that'll warm your feet, Miss
Spencer. I expect you caught a chill out there yesterday
in the yard."

"I haven't been in the yard for days."

She gave me a queer startled look. Perhaps I am now
forgetting what happened yesterday or the day before,

but I have no memory of going out. Everything here is materialistic and physical. It would never occur to Rose that I am in a spiritual crisis. It's my *mental* health that has been affected by Standish's death. I appear to be in a state of turmoil and even panic.

I wonder whether the Thornhill girl has come and been told that I can't see anyone at present? Otherwise it seems strange that she has not come. I trusted her. It is strange that I am not weeping at all. Something is locked inside me, too deep to find the ease of tears. At times it feels like a whirlwind and I am drowning. I feel lost, abandoned, as if the whole of my life had been a long betrayal that led me to this.

Why am I being punished? It is a stark question. I ask it many times, but no one will ever answer. I feel that nothing I can do now will ever work. I am like a leper. What I touch is infected, so by trying to help him I deprived Standish of death on his terms, infected his death in some terrible way, so he died in an ambulance. What could be more forlorn? Carried away like a corpse in a hearse.

What is happening to me? When I reread what I have written here, it is clear that, far from making myself whole as I imagined might be done (that was the challenge before me) I am sinking into madness or despair, fragmented, disoriented even when I try to find comfort in the past. Is it possible that a mind can quite suddenly fall to pieces? A sort of explosion as when all the petals of a flower suddenly fall? But if so, would I be aware of it? Does madness know itself as mad?

I must somehow get under this panic to solid ground.

Misery lives in me like a cancer. It is the misery of self-hatred and self-doubt. Why did I never marry? Selfishness? Some immaturity that was never ready for that lifetime commitment?

"Brightness falls from the air . . ."

What do I take with me into the darkness now? What am I? A bundle of fears and guilt, a spoiled child, whose every action reeks of self-involvement . . . Who can forgive me? Who will listen? To whom can I speak? Poor Richard Thornhill would be horrified by the depth of my depravity. He thinks of me, no doubt, as a poor dear old lady, white as the driven snow. But I am *black* inside, Mr. Thornhill, if you only knew! What is awful is to hate so much. There are times when I dream only of hitting Harriet hard across her mean, self-indulgent, lying mouth.

If keepers are corrupted by having absolute power, what about those they keep? We learn to ingratiate ourselves, to pretend we do not notice the slights and humiliations. Or we close ourselves off into that terrible place of anger, of rage and despair where Standish died. Is that my way? Is that what is now happening to me?

"Forgive us our trespasses as we forgive those who trespass against us." That crucial sentence looms ahead of me now when I say the Lord's Prayer. I try to believe, in this turmoil, that my only salvation is to think a great deal about where I myself have failed and fail every day.

Trying to assert myself as a child, I took advantage of John, and at least once allowed him to be punished for something I had done. And in those last months, was I generous to Ginny? Did I make any real effort to adapt myself to her needs and to their life together? I did not. When John and I played Scrabble, as we did by the hour, she was pushed aside, and I pretended that I couldn't play bridge (it has always bored me) so that we would not have to get in a fourth for endless bridge games. I did it out of snobbism. I wanted her to feel that John and I share an intellectual world she cannot enter. Then there were the sharp political arguments, resuming the old wars when we were growing up. She was right when she begged me to lay off. "John gets tired," she said once. "He's not up to your fierce tone." Of course those arguments exhausted me also. At least once I had to lie down because my heart was beating that queer irregular beat. But I paid no attention, blind to her kindness where John is concerned, walled in by arrogance and contempt. The fact is that I have become dreadfully selfish—perhaps I always was. I feel I was fighting for my pride as a human being, that to survive their atmosphere I had to impose mine on them. So if I am punished, I deserve it.

Yet I can never become gentle here—gentle or loving. Standish was the only one I could practice gentleness on, or love. I hold myself together with anger, and perhaps also with a sense of being an outsider and wishing to remain so. What have I to do with such vulgarity, such crude horror? Must I take it in? Is that what is asked of me? . . . I am too tired to write any more today. Perhaps I can go to sleep now. The nights are so bad, but for some reason my nap in the afternoon is a different, gentler kind of sleep. It is so wonderful to slip slowly into unconsciousness after resting my eyes on the cows and the field, as if I could in some way lie down myself on the sweet grass and be a contented animal for a change—the sleep of exhaustion. Let the mind go, Caro—what use is it to you now? A machine that is running down and can only make an occasional sputter, never really get on the road. Or, as they say (it has always amused me as an expression) "cook with gas."

I didn't get a rest after all. Harriet, very *affairée,* came to tell me she could wash my hair. She is leaving in two days, it appears, off to Florida with her lover. A Mrs. Close, a farmer's wife, will come to help out. Harriet was rough with me, pushed my head down too hard into the basin and at one point I thought I would suffocate. The true nature of a person is communicated as much, perhaps even more, by touch than by the look in his eyes. That is something I have learned here. I am not sure whether Harriet is so rough because she feels hatred toward me, or whether it is her natural way of being. Her hands have no gentleness in them. She pulled my hair when she was rinsing it, so hard I cried out once.

"You're hurting!"

"Not grateful, are you? When I took my hour off to do this!" She was suddenly furious and left me to dry it myself with a much too small towel. I finally went out and sat in the sun, shaking with emotion. I felt I had suffered

an assault on my person. When I came in Jack made a su-
preme effort to tell me—I find him so hard to decipher as
he gurgles rather than speaks—that my "friend," the
Thornhill girl, had come again and been told to go away
while Harriet was washing my hair. He shook his head
several times as if to say, "not good, what they did."

So my worst fears are being realized. The door that
had opened a crack is being slammed shut. Only there is
the faint hope that Mrs. Close, Harriet's replacement, will
fail to receive this ukase from on high. Rose, with her
mother here, would never have dared let Lisa in. Pa-
tience, Caro!

Yet why indulge in hope? Quite possibly the time has
passed for me to be helped by anyone from "outside"—
even dear Eva, should they manage to get her here. I am
beginning to feel beaten down in a new way, as if resili-
ence were slowly leaking away through these petty miser-
ies like salt in the coffee. What I am afraid of is that no
one would believe me if I tried to tell what is happening.
It sounds crazy to accuse someone of putting salt in one's
coffee! They are building up an image of me for the
world at large that will brainwash anyone who tries to
come close. That explains my feelings of turmoil and
panic—*that* explains it and not my idea of past guilt that
has to be expiated. I feel immense relief to have the clue.
Yes, I am afraid of a torture far worse than petty harass-
ments, the torture of not being *believed*. I am afraid of
being driven mad.

What if Lisa is persuaded that it *is* bad for me and de-
presses me to have visitors at present? Then if she herself

really wants to come—and how do I know?—she will re-
frain out of kindness. Richard Thornhill said he would
believe me and that I could trust him . . . but for how
long? How easy it is to tell half-truths that distort the
truth sometimes more dreadfully even than lies. I do get
stirred up by any visit. That is true and the half-truth is
to extrapolate this into a suggestion that therefore visits
must cease, that they are bad for me. The only person
who can be called "well" in this establishment is he who
is totally passive; anyone who "resists" is mad and dan-
gerous.

And so I am back again, battering my heart against the
absence of God, against the terrible need to be comforted
by this imaginary Father who knows the fall of a sparrow
but who allowed Standish to die in extreme indignity,
alone. "For Thine is the power . . ." God created the cat
who devours the sparrow. If He is the power, why do the
wicked flourish? Why are the old disposed of in places
like this? "Who cares?" is the ceaseless cry of those in
Hell. It is absurd to believe for a moment that it is in the
divine purpose to prevent the old from ripening toward
death in a fruitful way. If we believe in God, then we
have to believe equally in a power sometimes stronger
than His and in a kingdom other than His, in evil more
potent than we have faced before. Of course this is what
came to us through the concentration camps. If God was
not there, then who *was* there? *Christ Stopped at Eboli*,
and the village described in the book of that title was de-
picted as a misery beyond good or evil. Standish's cry
that day when Richard Thornhill was here (how long

ago? It seems an eternity) that God never got further than the village store said the same thing, exactly. Are there those beyond the dominion of God, outside it? Am I among them now?

I will write a letter to Richard Thornhill and see if I can persuade Mrs. Close—close to God? Close to the devil?—to see that it gets mailed.

"And what's all that writing for?" Harriet asked when she came in with my supper, dead-tasting frozen haddock with a congealed cream sauce over it and a boiled potato.

"A game of solitaire," I answered. "I'll need some new copybooks soon—decks of cards, you might call them."

She sniffed and went out. So, to my letter,

Late September

Dear Mr. Thornhill,

I need some copybooks for the journal I am keeping. It is a necessity or I would not ask. They have told your daughter I do better without visitors at present. That is a lie. It is true that I am very depressed. Depression is natural to anyone in my situation. I am being punished for telling you what I did and for the inspectors who came. All I ask now is to be believed.

Yours very sincerely.

But when I reread that letter, it sounded so desperate —even mad—that I shall wait some days before I send it, and probably decide then to hold it back. I am learning that any true cry from the heart of an old person creates too much havoc in a listener, is too disturbing, because nothing can really be done to help us on the downward path. So, mentioning the horror of growing old alone becomes an intolerable burden. There seem to be only a few responses possible. One is the dreadful false comfort of the cliché, "It can't be as bad as all that" or "Things will surely be better tomorrow, dear." (I suffer excruciatingly from endearments that are casual and perfunctory, because I am so starved for real feelings, for love itself, I suppose. My mother used to call me "Dear heart" and Alex called me "Lamb of God," I can't imagine why. I am and always was very unlike a lamb. My father called me "Kiddo," I suddenly remember—how old-fashioned that does sound!)

The most cruel response to a *cri de coeur* is not to believe it, or to pretend that it is a lie. That is Harriet's weapon, or one of them. "You just imagine you can't sleep, dear. I heard you snoring at four this morning." There is also the cajoling response, the one that treats the old person as an infant, the "Now, now, quiet down" sort of thing. "I'll bring you some tea."

One could only be answered differently by true caring, and that, I suspect, would show itself in silence, by the quality of listening or some shy gesture of love.

Old age is really a disguise that no one but the old themselves see through. I feel exactly as I always did, as young inside as when I was twenty-one, but the outward shell conceals the real me—sometimes even from itself— and betrays that person deep down inside, under wrinkles and liver spots and all the horrors of decay. I sometimes think that I feel things *more* intensely than I used to, not less. But I am so afraid of appearing ridiculous. People expect serenity of the old. That is the stereotype, the mask we are expected to put on. But how many old people *are* serene? I have known one or two. My granny was, but my grandfather, my father's father, became very violent and irascible. I was terrified of him and my father dreaded going to see him. He was forever going to court about some supposed slight or slander. He was a newspaper man, owner of a small-town newspaper for which he wrote most of the editorials, and by the time he died had squandered half his fortune, never very large, on perfectly absurd lawsuits.

My anger, because I am old, is considered a sign of madness or senility. Is this not cruel? Are we to be deprived even of righteous anger? Is even irritability to be treated as a "symptom"? There I go—and I myself have just accused Granddad of becoming violent when he was *old!* Was he not violent before? Of course I don't know, as I only knew him when he was past seventy, but I suspect that he always was, only it seemed outrageous in the old man as it had not seemed when he was young and "fiery."

How *expression* relieves the mind! I feel quite lively and myself again just because I have managed to write two pages of dissent about old age! Among all the other deprivations here we are deprived of *expression*. The old men slowly atrophy because no one asks them what they feel or why. Could they speak if someone did? And why haven't I tried? I look at them from very far away as if they were in the distance, across a wide river. We have nothing in common. Why pretend that we do?

I cannot quite believe in the miracle of Mrs. Close. The miracle has happened since Harriet took off two days ago, and I am stretched out on my bed like a swimmer who, near exhaustion, can lie on a beach and rest at last. The whole atmosphere has changed radically since this angelic person made her appearance in a clean white apron over a blue and white checked dress like some character in a Beatrix Potter book. My fingers tingle with pleasure at the very thought of describing her—her quick silent feet, her work-hardened hands that are so full of wisdom and gentleness when she does the slightest thing, and above all, her round, soft, pink face and her quiet gray eyes, observant, humorous, discreet. At first she simply set silently to *work*, cleaned the whole house as it has never before been cleaned, even washed the hall floor! There was a pink tray cloth on my tray this morning (where did she ever find it?) and a pink rose in a little glass.

"Anything more I can do for you, Miss Spencer?" she asked, and she did not hurry off without listening.

I would like to have kept her close to me all day, to smell her *clean* smell, as if some heavenly nurse had come to be with me. But of course she is fearfully busy. Rose follows her around making acid comments. "You don't have to do that, Mrs. Close. They don't notice." She pays no attention and does what she wants to do. And I think Rose is daunted by the sheer speed and efficiency at work.

Later in the morning I heard laughter from the old men—amazing! And when she brought in my lunch, we had a little talk. She was pleased because I recognized the rose as a Queen Elizabeth. She had picked it early this morning in her garden, she told me.

"Sit down, Mrs. Close," I begged her, "just for a minute."

"Well," she hesitated. "I will if you want me to."

"You've done a marvelous job here this morning. We're spic and span."

We could hear Rose clattering dishes in the kitchen, and Mrs. Close whispered, "It's a disgrace, Miss Spencer . . . the dirt . . ."

"It's more than the dirt," I ventured.

"I know," and we exchanged a look, the look between two women who understand each other. The relief of that! Indescribable relief. I was too moved to speak, but she saw the tears in my eyes, took my hand in both of hers, and gave it a squeeze. It was not a sentimental gesture at all. It *affirmed* our humanity and regard for each other.

"You shouldn't be here," she said. "It's not the place for you or the likes of you."

"If someone comes and asks for me, you won't send

them away, will you?" I whispered. There might not be another chance to get this across.

"Of course not. Are you expecting relatives?"

"A friend, Miss Thornhill."

Then Rose called out in her harsh voice, "Mrs. Close! Mrs. Close! The trays are waiting."

I must be very careful not to antagonize Rose—not to do anything that could poison this reprieve. Harriet will be away for two whole weeks, maybe more, who knows? Meanwhile I am alive in a way I have not been since I came. That is what a mere presence, if it is kind, can do. There is something to look forward to. I shall wake up thinking that Mrs. Close will be coming in to say good morning.

It is only a little frightening to be swept back into feeling so much. Don't make a fool of yourself, Caro! Old people, we are told, get infatuated easily. I understand it all so much better than I would have even five years ago. Whatever lives in us, the heart and its capacity for suffering and for joy never dies, and must have an object. The sin would be to stop loving. But I have only seen this dear woman for a day and already I feel less starved and ornery, less arid, less ready to break out in anger. A single rose, a tray cloth, the presence of goodheartedness, of imagination—now I am ready for Lisa. I know that I can still respond to life in a normal human way. I am not disintegrating into madness.

The rose has opened during the day. I have lain here for an hour really paying attention to it. And now I think I'll go and sit outdoors.

People have remissions from cancer when for a time they feel quite well. I am being given a remission from despair and decline. It may be my last chance to recover and sort out all that must be resolved, so I must use it well. Time had become slack, tedious. Now it races. But I am accomplishing quite a lot in my own nice quiet noisy way. Who used to say that? "Nice quiet noisy way" . . . My Aunt Isabel, of course! She was the black sheep of the family, not only went to college but got a Ph.D. in political science. At a time when ladies neither drank nor smoked she did both with zest, and I suppose she was the only person in the family with whom I could feel wholly at ease. She even made a trip to London to meet Alex and approved of our liaison. How strange that I have not thought of her since I came here. I suppose it was feeling myself again that has made it possible. The very thought of her energy and the great way she died, of a heart attack on the way to get an honorary degree from the University of Wisconsin, would have depressed me too much when I first landed here. I never quite met her standards of superior achievement, but at least she understood why a woman of some intellectual distinction might hesitate to marry. "Be yourself, Caro," she used to say. "No one can be that for you." She was a prima donna, of course, and of course the family resented her fame and her women friends, her getting away with murder and flourishing despite it all.

She was my mother's older sister; they could not have been more different. When she came to visit we had a family joke that Hurricane Isabel was about to strike. She arrived with huge amounts of luggage, two or three briefcases of papers and books, made demands no other woman would have been allowed to make, worked till the early morning hours after everyone else was asleep, got up at eleven and expected breakfast, demanded endless martinis before dinner, teased my father and treated my mother with what can only be called condescension. But when Hurricane Isabel left, the house seemed very empty and life rather dull, even to my parents. They resented her intensity, her drive, but without it, for a week or so, they saw the dingy aspects of their life rather too clearly. At least, if they did not, I *did*. I couldn't help comparing her life, so wide open, so luxuriant, with theirs, so closed in, prim and safe.

For years I was terribly jealous of John, in whom she took an interest. Children bored her and at fourteen and fifteen I was a rather boring child, no doubt. But John was interested in ideas, a worthy antagonist, and they went at it together. Often my parents went to bed in sheer desperation, while she and John went on talking about "progressive education" or whatever was in the air, and I, solemn ghost at the feast, nearly went to sleep but refused to leave for fear of missing something.

Later on I suppose I was a little in love with her and her life, and later on she enjoyed what she called my toughmindedness, teased me about being a mathematician, took me one wonderful summer to Europe, a slow, rich progress to her favorite places—Chartres, of course,

the Dordogne, St. Paul de Vence, Venice, and finally
Sion, in Switzerland. What would she have been like if
she had lived to be very old? When she began to lose her
powers? Well, of course, faithful Daphne, the last one of
her several "friends," would have looked out for her. She
attracted people like a magnet, attracted by sheer vitality
and zest for life. She was always surrounded by admiring
students, male and female. And by women, jealous of
each other. I do not believe, strangely enough, that she
was a very passionate woman. She aroused passions
rather than experiencing them, is my guess. Oh, what I
wouldn't give to have her sail in here and demolish the
place by the sheer force of her personality! She would
have carried me off without a moment's hesitation!—Such
fantasies, Caro. The truth is that the people who could
save the old in places like this have died—that is why we
are put here, because there *is* no one.

I had a note, at long last, from Ginny to apologize for
the long lapse. John, it seems, has been quite ill with
pleurisy and nearly died. So that explains that. She prom-
ises to come in before they go south later on. He cannot,
say the doctors, stand the winter here. The winter! I
think of it with dread. Snow piled against the windows,
drafts, being marooned.

Well, I was sitting outdoors, reading, at peace with my-
self, when Richard Thornhill drove up late that after-

noon. He brought four or five splendid copybooks and a powerful transistor radio on which he thinks I can get music at certain hours. It has an earphone thing so I can listen without disturbing anyone. He brought more flowers from his wife. But, far more precious, he sat down for an hour and we had a real talk. I am almost afraid of so many good things happening—what fury stands in the wings? It can't last. A gentle voice, gentle hands, the silent communion with Mrs. Close *and* a charming young man who treats me with respect and listens to what I say! Can all this be real?

Richard (we are on a first-name basis now, at least on my side; he cannot quite bring himself to call me Caro) asked why they had told Lisa I couldn't see her—was it by my wish?

"No, that was Harriet's way of punishing me for having told you so much, for the inspectors coming."

"I can't believe it!" The words sprang out spontaneously. He had no idea how frightful they were to hear. I had a queer sensation of dizziness and covered my eyes with one hand. It all rushed in, the fear of madness, of not being believed. I didn't know what to say, how to tell him. But he must have guessed, for he added after a moment, "Of course I believe you, Miss Spencer, if you tell me so."

But his eyes were troubled when I met them.

"No one believes in wickedness until he meets it face to face. I never did before." I was trembling and could hardly light my cigarette. He took the lighter from my hand and did it for me.

"Please, Miss Spencer, don't be upset. I had no idea, of course, that my effort to help could go wrong."

"It didn't . . . only . . . you see they took Standish away and he died such a lonely death in the ambulance. I felt responsible. The inspectors won't allow really sick people here any more. And that's right. Only *they* hate me now."

It was an awful moment. I felt I was spoiling his visit for him and for me, too. Tears flew down my cheeks like rain. I couldn't help it. "Nothing can be changed here," I managed to say when I had pulled myself together. "It's a locked world."

"It doesn't have to be," he said firmly. "Next time Lisa comes she will force her way in. Of *that* I can assure you."

For me it had been a violent fall back into the grief I had kept at bay since Standish died. But with it came a flash of insight. I did not, of course, tell Richard what I saw in that flash. It was that things can be changed here, but only by violent action. If I lose my temper I will be put in the dark again. But if I burn the place down some day, I can open this locked world—at least to death by fire, better than death by bad smells and bedpans and lost minds in sordidly failing bodies. I was staggered by the flash of what I conceived. The tears stopped at once and I became crazily cheerful, talked a blue streak, told him about John, gave a quite humorous criticism of the long novel he had brought, as a strong but aberrant cartoon of life—what people want to believe, not what is true.

[89

And this led us back to old age and death. And finally to my King Charles' Head, wickedness, and what one does in its presence, how one handles it.

"People become wicked," I said in the flush of all this talk, "when they have absolute power. I think that's the answer. One reads about fathers who brutalize infants, for instance. 'The battered child syndrome,' I believe it is called. Have you run into it, Richard? It seems so horrible."

"Yes," he nodded. "It happens every day. A man or woman is frustrated for some reason, an unfair boss, or what have you—comes home to a crying baby and breaks its arm. I've seen it."

"What do you do about it? How can one help?"

"I don't know," he sighed. "I try never to blame, or at least try to withhold blame, try to understand what the frustrations back of cruelty are. It's never easy, Miss Spencer. Such people are eaten by guilt."

"My experience of wickedness is that it is Protean—you can't seize onto it. And you can't because the truly wicked perhaps live in Heaven, a Heaven of their own making. They do not admit even to themselves what they have done or are doing. Harriet Hatfield is a perfect example. Her image of herself, I feel sure, is that of a compassionately overworked human being who has taken over the responsibility of others toward their fathers, mothers, sisters, et cetera, for little pay. She feels superior to me, for instance, *because* I have been left in her care. In her own eyes she is perfectly good. *She* feels no guilt, I can assure you. It is the innocent, not the guilty, who live

in Hell," I heard myself say. And I have been thinking
about this ever since. (The wonderful thing about real
conversation is that it stimulates one to new insights.)
Richard fumbled when I pressed my point, "And if that is
so, how can you believe in a just God?"

I liked him because he took his time. He narrowed his
eyes and looked down at the hands clasping his crossed
knee. He is rather an elegant creature and I enjoy looking
at him. He pleases me as a man and as a human being.
Brilliance, intellectually speaking, is not required of the
ministry, but integrity is. And it is becoming rare in any
field. Richard has it, and I feel it in Lisa too.

"You are really probing my faith, Miss Spencer," he
said with an odd shy smile.

"I suppose so. Well?"

"I don't know," and he suddenly laughed. "Perhaps
part of me believes that we are every day making God
possible as He made us possible—He fails us when we fail
Him. Maybe," he said, "wickedness is what God cannot
deal with Himself. We have to deal with it."

"Cancer, for instance," I murmured, "when normal cells
go wild and overmultiply—you mean we can't blame God
for that?"

"Maybe . . ."

It was time to change the subject and I did. But it has
given me much to think about. In this little distance from
Harriet and in the blessed presence of Mrs. Close, I must
try to achieve detachment and to stop hating so much.
Hate is corrosive. But how to deal with Harriet? That re-
mains a mystery.

These are wonderful days. They begin with dear Anna Close and my breakfast tray—though actually they begin with sunrise. Sometimes the field is covered with frost and sparkles when the sun climbs over the trees. I lie in my bed as the grey dawn changes to blue and the round red sun climbs up. Frost has brought changes to the trees and now everything is red and gold at the end of the field. I do not really want to die at all these days. I am avid for life. Sometimes Anna can sit down for a minute after my breakfast when she has taken care of the old men and comes back to get my tray. She is not a talker. I feel perfectly at peace when she is there and we do not need words. She seems to understand me in a way I have needed for years. The room feels airy and clean when she has been there with her magic touch. No more dust under the bureau these days! But it is not that, it is being cared for as though I were worthy of care. It is being not humiliated but treasured.

"I wish I could take you home with me," she said the other day, "but my husband wouldn't hear of it, and there are no conveniences. Children pouring in and out."

"Don't let's think ahead," I said quickly. I wanted to ask her when Harriet is due back, but I was afraid to. The only way I can handle this inevitable disaster is not to think about it. "Let's count our blessings," I added. "You make me feel ten years younger, Anna."

That made her laugh her soft secret laugh. "I'm sure I can't think why. I'm no one for the likes of you, a plain farmer's wife who has never been outside the state, if you can believe it."

"It's not that," I said, brushing away what seems quite irrelevant. "You're an angel in disguise."

"Quite a disguise, I must say," and she laughed again and gave me an amused look out of her clear blue eyes.

I think she is a little afraid of my feeling for her. No doubt it seems absurd. And no doubt it is. But while she is here, surely I am permitted to bask in goodness—it will not last long in this place. She insists on taking my things home to wash so they won't be stuffed into the machine here. She brings them back beautifully ironed and wrapped in tissue paper. "I do like that blouse," she will say, giving the package a pat. "It has a label from Paris." I realize that a blouse from Paris dazzles her.

"Hermès," I murmur.

"I just can't understand their leaving you here," she says. For by now of course she knows all about Ginny and John. "It's all very well for those old men, this is the sort of place they lived in before. But *you* . . ."

"Nobody stays special when they're old, Anna. That's what we have to learn."

"I don't believe that." She is, for once, angry, and flushes. "I would like to wring that Ginny's neck."

But now I am defended I can be generous. "It's not her fault, you know. She's got her hands full. And I was beastly to her, so maybe I deserve what I got."

So we talk, but it is not the words that matter. When

she goes she pats my hand and sometimes kisses me on the cheek. "You'd better get outside in the warm sun," she says, "and do your writing there."

My notebooks fascinate her. "What do you do it for?" she asked me once.

"Oh, to keep alive, I suppose—to tell myself I am still able to feel and think." But there is another reason. The notebooks are my touchstone for sanity.

Anna's mother died last year. She was completely blotto for years, at the end didn't know who Anna was. When Anna tells me about her, I get terribly frightened. She turned against them all before the end and threw things. And Anna had a hard time keeping her at home for her husband had enough of it long before the end. He appears to be a rather hard man, hard but a man of integrity, nearly works himself to death with the cows. They still have a herd, and when Anna comes here at seven she has been up since five to give him his breakfast. He didn't want her to take the job, but finally agreed because they need a new frigidaire and her weeks here helping out will make the downpayment. I sometimes ask myself what I do for her, she who does so much for me. I think perhaps it is a glimpse of a woman's life not entirely spent in physical struggle to keep going—pretty things, a blouse from Hermès. She does not want them for herself, but she gets a romantic delight out of what I am and plies me with questions about Europe. To her I suppose I am like some rare bird, a scarlet tanager who suddenly appears in the back yard. One day she asked me, "Why didn't you marry, lovely as you are?"

It was a hard question to answer. How could I tell her, perhaps that I am a failure, couldn't take what it would have cost to give up an authentic being, myself, to take in the stranger? That I failed because I was afraid of losing myself when in fact I might have grown through sharing an equality with another human being. And yet . . . do I really regret not marrying? No, to be quite honest, *no*. I must have been silent for some time, because she said, "I shouldn't have asked."

"I'm sorry, I was thinking," I answered.

"You don't have to tell me."

"I want to tell you the truth. That's the problem. What is the truth?"

But then she had to go, for Rose was calling her as usual. Rose deeply resents our intimacy. She senses, I suppose, that something is going on that cannot be controlled. But even Rose has become more human in Harriet's absence. She dislikes me because she senses a superiority I cannot hide however much I try to. But I do not believe she actually hates me as Harriet does. She is simply at a loss about how to behave toward me. She has been trained to treat the inmates as inferiors to be ordered about, controlled in every possible way. I escape the control simply by being myself. However meek I am, I am still myself. This, I presume, is what has to be destroyed.

I live in dread of Anna's leaving, but there is something I can keep. Quite often I can get real music on the transistor radio in the evenings. It makes what used to be

long hours after Anna has gone home a time of marvels. I
marvel that such beauty flows in through my ears, un-
heard by anyone else. What a miracle! Last night I heard
the Fauré Requiem, sung by the boys' voices in King's
Chapel, and the other night Mozart's clarinet quintet and
a Beethoven quartet. I have never listened to music with
such absolute attention in a long life of hearing a great
deal of it. Here there is nothing to distract. I give myself
wholly to listening as if an astonishing angel had come
into the room. I force myself not to daydream, not to
think about Anna, for instance. Giving the music my
whole attention I sometimes actually see notes written on
a page (a curious reversal of the usual thing of hearing
what one sees). I get a distilled pleasure from it that re-
sembles what mathematics did for me in the past—a total
absorption in abstract beauty, I suppose it is. My feelings
have nothing to do with this pleasure, at least when I am
hearing music. The romantics, even Beethoven occasion-
ally, have a less wholesome effect. There is the danger
that the Vox Humana sound too loudly, and then some
door into private never-solved conflict flies open and I am
undone. I become a lover, not a listener. Who was it who
said that Mozart *feels* like an angel? Perhaps Gide in the
journals. That is not quite right, but my understanding of
what Gide meant is clear nonetheless. Mozart always
transcends the dung of human experience. It is all there
but transcended, as, indeed, an angel might apprehend it.
And does that mean detachment? Perhaps, but of a very
special kind known only to the creators. I would like to
write a poem for Anna. But in this strange time of my

life, in this strange place, it appears that I must suffer
feeling without expression—it is to be used, if at all, as a
reason for not dying. And I am not a poet, God knows.

But I am about to die. Harriet comes back on Satur-
day, in three days, in seventy-two hours. When Anna told
me this morning my breakfast tray had a deep red rose
on it. I went absolutely blank and turned my head away.
I was falling through space in a state of uncontrollable
panic. I could feel the sweat on my upper lip.

"Are you all right, dear?"

I was unable to answer. I was afraid that a single word,
even "yes," even "no," would open a floodgate, that I
would cling to her like a baby and howl. Perhaps Anna
sensed that the best thing was to leave me alone. I lis-
tened to her gentle cheerful voice talking to the old men,
their murmurs and cackles like a crowd of starlings.

How can I handle Anna's leaving? It was always there,
the darkness ahead, but until the time of Harriet's return
had become definite, circumscribed, I could pretend that
she might be killed in an automobile accident. I could in-
dulge in fantasies. Two weeks is a very short reprieve for
those in Hell. A two weeks holiday, one might say. I can-
not imagine a way to get myself ready for what must
come. I suppose it is a matter of closing the door. Batten-
ing myself down. My jaw aches from holding a grief
back. And I cannot summon the courage to get up and

dress. It is all very well to scold myself, "Don't be absurd, Caro," but reason tells me that it is a disaster, a real one. It cannot really be transcended.

When Anna came back at eleven with a glass of milk and a biscuit I asked whether she would come and see me "afterwards." Her words were reassuring but I saw the shadow of a doubt cross her candid eyes—would she be allowed to?

"Anyway I could write to you, couldn't I?"

"Yes, dear, of course."

"And will you answer?"

She looked daunted, for once at a loss. I could see that the idea of putting feeling into written words was disturbing. "I'm not very good at writing letters," she said with that secret smile that hovers about her lips as though she were about to say something that will never be said. "My son James laughed at me when he got back from Vietnam last year. Apparently all I ever said was, 'I miss you and come home soon.' I'll try, dear," she said quickly, "but you mustn't expect too much."

"But you will read my letters?"

"Of course." For a second our eyes met. Then she fumbled for words, "I think so much of you, Miss Spencer . . . you must know I do."

So I am busy making up letters. That is something to hold onto. How very strange that at seventy-six in a relationship with an inarticulate person who cannot put any of it into words, I myself am on the brink of understanding things about love I have never understood before. But then I remind myself that this is one of the proofs of true

love: It always comes as revelation, and we approach it
always with awe as if it had never taken place before on
earth in any human heart, for the very essence of its
power is that it makes all things new.

Have I ever before really understood the power and
the healing grace of sensitive hands like Anna's? Have I
ever experienced *loving* as I do in one glance from her
amazing clear eyes that take in at once what my needs
are, whether it be food or a gentle caress, a pillowcase
changed, a glass of warm milk? No wonder so many old
men fall in love with their nurses! I used to think of them
with contempt—old babies, old self-indulgent babies. And
now here I am in much the same plight! But I cannot
offer Anna marriage or take her into my life, or in any
way help her as she helps me. I cannot bind her to me.

Oh dear, that is what makes the separation so
agonizing—our mode of expression will be gone. She will
forget me soon enough, no doubt. She is still carried for-
ward on the demands of day-to-day living. I am frozen
here in this "still pond, no more moving."

And I am crying again and cannot go on.

Yesterday I was unable to write, but I did get up, made
myself dress and go out, though the air was chilly. It was
lucky I did because Lisa came, and I can always talk
more easily outside this jail. She came, bless her heart, to
say that she has arranged to bring Eva here next week,

and she must have seen what a tonic effect that news
had, something to look forward to after the disaster to-
morrow. I am quite proud of myself because I did not
break down. It is odd how *not* crying makes my whole
jaw ache. But I must try to appear at least to be normal. I
want this girl to believe in my sanity. It is quite necessary
for my future plan that she do so. I asked her quite ca-
sually whether she could bring me a large can of lighter
fluid when she comes next week—she brought me a car-
ton of cigarettes and a crossword puzzle book.

(I didn't tell her that ever since a very rough passage to
Europe, years ago, when I did crossword puzzles be-
tween bouts of seasickness, I can't look at a crossword
puzzle without my stomach heaving.)

It is a comfort to have a plan that would end the Hell
here but the strange thing is that the very existence of
Anna (even though I shall see her rarely if ever), the fact
of pure human goodness having come into the orbit,
makes it harder to do anything drastic now. And perhaps
it was her presence, shaking out a mop as we talked, giv-
ing me a wave of her hand in the doorway, that made it
possible for me to get Lisa to talk a little about her world,
as shaken by love as mine is, avid for food that will nour-
ish that hunger—poetry, music. Her young man has gone
to Turkey this summer, the mecca for youth these days, a
kind of new world where they imagine they are Marco
Polo all over again, bumming rides to cross mountains
and deserts to Katmandu—I think she said Katmandu.
She is afraid of losing him to the wandering girls, to the
pick-ups, afraid of his losing his way. He had wanted to

be a doctor, she said, but was wavering now before the arduous years of training.

"Peter is very young," she said, as women have said of their lovers from time immemorial. She seemed rather an old-fashioned girl this time, and I teased her and told her she had better go to Turkey herself.

"I'd be scared to death," she admitted, a quick wild blush rising to her ears. "I'm not adventurous."

"He'll be back with the winter birds," I told her. "You'll see."

With this visit I climbed out of that pit of panic and loneliness. It gave me back a sense of proportion. It's too easy in this place to go a little crazy as prisoners often do. The inner world blows up like a balloon. But now I can rest. I must prepare to say goodbye to Anna and do it with dignity. Compose the mind, Caro! Think of goodness. Think of courage. Think of all you know that a young girl cannot know, and be strong.

Words . . . words . . . words . . . I reread that last passage and it was dust and ashes.

Harriet has been back for two days. She is full of hearty cheer and hatred. I suppose she hated to come back as much as we dreaded her return. She is brown and has lost a little weight. The first morning she brought in my tray, the old plastic one, as before, she greeted me with "I hear you've been spoiled, Miss Spencer, but you must understand that I have no time for fol-de-rols."

"I understand," I said meekly. I am terribly afraid of her, irrationally afraid. I feel like an animal that growls at some perfect stranger as if meanness and cruelty had an actual smell. But I do not dare growl. The mean mistress has to be placated if possible.

"Did you have a good holiday?" I managed to ask.

"Good enough, but everything is so expensive, how can a person have any fun?"

I wanted to say, if you mean sex, that usually does not cost money, but I refrained. I suppose she pays for her lover, but perhaps it is mean-spirited of me to think so. At any rate she dominates Ned completely, and he looks exhausted. She is always cajoling him into doing some odd job. He comes home from the day's work—a mechanic, I think he said he was—looking as if all he wanted was a beer and some peace and quiet. Instead I hear her shouting at him, "You haven't been emptying bedpans all day! Take out the rubbish and stop babying yourself!" He never talks back. They have sex, as the saying goes, but it doesn't look as though they had much else.

I breathe Anna in and out with each breath. Her name is my air. And today I reread all I had written about her coming, the miracle that it was. But I am very sore inside as if I had been beaten. So sometimes "breathing Anna" is breathing pain.

My daily stint is to endure. It is different from conflict. Conflict may be fruitful, at least it contains in it the seeds of a future, of a resolution. I endure in a vacuum. What I endure will not end ever until my death. When I wake up I still imagine I will see Anna, that her smile will soon

come to me, and then I have to realize that the good
dream is over and the nightmare is the reality. The early
morning is the hardest time. I can hardly bear to see the
sun rise, to see the golden leaves sifting down, down,
down, and to know that I have to get through a whole
long day. So I get up and dress. Today I cleaned my
room myself, to no praise, I may say.

"What do you think you're doing with that dustpan?"
Harriet asked irritably. "Isn't it clean enough for you
here?"

"I just felt like doing it."

"Mind your own business, Miss Spencer. Please give
me that dirt and I'll dispose of it."

Unfortunately it is too cold today to sit outside. Per-
haps I can manage a little walk later on. But first I want
to write a letter to Anna—I have waited two days to do it,
two long days. I felt unable. And even now my hand
shakes when I take the pen. It is as though I were some-
how contaminated already, not the person she knew.
Hatred seeps in, the fear of madness. Anna, help me.

I will try a letter out and see what happens. But words
are no help. She is not a word-person. She is back in her
own life now. What did I mean to her? She is "outside,"
safe. I am inside, in danger of despair and madness, in
danger of appearing ridiculous—even to myself.

Yet I must believe. I must try to keep intact what is
gentle and loving—as long as that is possible. So I lie here
on my bed and look out at the sky, pure and brilliant, the
wholesome world outdoors, where there are seasons, the
leaves change and fall. . . . The chipmunks are busy

these days. I love to watch their swift runs, tail in air—
they are harvesting. And I must harvest, too, stow some-
where in the depths of my heart all I have been given to
sustain me, all I can keep of Anna. And give her all I can
summon today to tell her what she has given me. . . .

End of September

Dearest Anna,

You have been gone now for two days. And I have
wanted to write you. I hope that you miss me sometimes,
although I am sure your own life has filled in whatever
emptiness you may have experienced at first. It is differ-
ent for me, of course. I do not lead a normal life any
longer and so, perhaps, am not quite normal myself. You
may think I am a loon when you read this, yet I must try
to trust you. You are the only person whom I can trust
now. Lisa came and told me she would bring me down to
see you next week if that is all right with you? You must
imagine how much I need your answer. I feel so hopeless.

I want to tell you that you have brought me back from
Hell to Heaven, from nothing but hatred and despair to
love. You must understand that this is a miracle. I shall
never forget your face, your gentle hands . . . I want to
tell you what touch can do to bring life back to the dead.
The first time you clasped my hand I became a little
child. I felt safe for the first time since I came to this
dreadful place. Every morning I woke before sunrise and
knew you were coming soon, I was filled with joy like a
child. When you were busy working I heard your voice.
The rose you had put on my tray was beside me. Of such
small things is Heaven made when one loves again. But

all the time I knew it was only for a little while. Perhaps
that is why my feelings were so intense. It all had to be
experienced immediately for it could not last. I wonder
whether you ever felt like this—that we had very little
time.

You gave me so much and I could give you so little,
that is what bothers me. But once you said you liked my
blouse from Hermès. I want to give it to you and when
Lisa brings me I'll have it with me. We won't be able to
talk at all, I fear.

I bought the blouse to please Alex, the man I loved. So
it comes from my old love to you, my miracle of new
love, with all my heart.

This letter says too much and too little. But I have
found it very hard to write. What we had was a *silent*
communion. Words are leaden by comparison. God bless
you and keep you, and do not forget that I love you.

Caro

I have read and reread this letter, so inadequate. But I
doubt whether I can do it better. I have to hold so much
back. I will copy it out this afternoon. Now I must go for
a walk, get *out*. Perhaps I can manage to walk this ache
out, get myself really physically tired.

Did I go for a walk? I don't even remember. I must
have, yes of course I did, for that was how Harriet got
hold of the letter. I had left the copybook open on my

bed. Since then—how many days?—I am being tortured.
Harriet read what I had written. She has made every-
thing dirty and destroyed it.

"I didn't know you were a dirty old woman," she said
when she brought my lunch in that day—when was it?—
"At least the old men think about women. They are not
filthy like you."

"It's not filthy to love Anna," I said. "She's a beautiful
person."

"And she kisses you, no doubt, and she clasps your
hand."

The sneers fell like stones, well aimed. Every one found
its mark. "This is no place for queers," she said. "We'll
have you in the State Hospital if you ever dare send such
a filthy letter."

I was silent—silent with dismay.

"At least I've saved Anna from your dirt," Harriet said
smugly. "She *is* a good wife and mother and grand-
mother. She doesn't need your smears, Miss Spencer."

How much was I supposed to take in silence? I got up
and walked out of the house. I felt I would walk till I
dropped dead. But they soon caught up with me in the
truck, she and her lover.

"Oh no, you don't run away," Harriet said as they came
to a halt and the man jumped out. "I undertook to take
care of you and I will."

Every word of this is grooved so deeply into my mind
that I write it down now, days later. I was put in the dark
when they got me back, and I suppose Lisa, if she came,
was sent away. Now they think I am tamed out of any re-

action, I am back in my bed. I am given light again. I am very meek and mild, of course.

Today I was handed a postcard from Ginny and John, from Forida. It said, "A bit hot here, but John is getting along nicely. We both send our love."

Love? I have come to loathe the word. I hope never to utter or to hear it again as long as I live.

Harriet holds over me the threat of commitment to the State Hospital, but I doubt if she would have the legal right. I suffered real panic about this and have lain low. But sometimes I long to be put out of my misery. At least there they have drugs. I would be put to sleep, I suppose, kept in a state of lethargy. Wouldn't that be better than my present anxiety—am I a dirty old woman?—guilt, and despair. I have spoken, I feel, lightly of despair before this episode. Now I know more about it. Now I begin to understand Standish. There is a point of no return, a point when the only question is whether to choose to starve to death or to use a more violent means.

The Lord's Prayer has ceased to be of any comfort. I cannot forgive my enemies. I have been murdered. Murdered in the most cruel of ways possible. How can I ever forgive Harriet? Why should I? If Richard comes I shall refuse to see him. I cannot offer him my humiliation or even talk about it. I have become a leper to myself. I cannot contaminate lovely innocent Lisa. I am beyond the pale. Very well—I have my own ideas of what those beyond the pale do—the blacks, for instance. They finally come to see that violence is the only answer to oppression. They make bombs. What was good in them becomes

evil. They want only to destroy. I understand them now
very well. I have been punished enough. Once I believed
in mercy and had a supreme example of it in one who
shall be nameless now. But mercy fails against wicked-
ness. God, if you exist, take me away. Blind me, destroy
my every sense, make me numb. Drive me mad. It is all I
can pray for now.

Days have gone by. It must be October, mid-October I
think, because the leaves are flying fast. The great maples
are skeletons against the sky. The beeches are still a mar-
velous greenish-yellow, a Chinese yellow, I have always
thought. Pansy, now the nights are cold, sometimes
comes to sleep with me, and slips out (clever cat) before
anyone has stirred. The only time I weep is when she is
there, purring beside me. I, who longed for touch, can
hardly bear the sweetness of that little rough tongue lick-
ing my hand.

There is nothing to say any longer. And I am writing
only because Lisa is to bring Eva today. Harriet doesn't
want them to see me as I was—dirty hair I hardly both-
ered to comb, an old woman, a grotesque miserable ani-
mal. She washed my hair and it is drying now. This time
she was gentle, thank God. I suppose she can be because
I am just a passive bundle. She brought me a clean and,
for once, properly ironed nightgown. I do not dress very
often any more. I feel safer in bed. I suspect they are put-

ting sedatives in my coffee, for I feel very sleepy after breakfast. I am too tired now to go on writing—anyway why go on? I once believed I could keep myself alive here, partly by recording the experience. But I had not reckoned with . . . but I simply must not think about that. The only thing a tortured being asks is not to be tortured any more. I wonder whether X—I shall never speak her name again—has tried to reach me. But who knows? I may have made the whole thing up. Mad people do have dreams, I suppose. Anyway, it was all such a long time ago, if it ever happened. How am I to hide my misery from Lisa, from Eva? How not to hurt them and hurt myself by spreading this leprosy? I do not address myself any more as Caro. Caro is dead. I cannot say "Pull yourself together, Caro," for that person has ceased to exist. Someone else, mentally ill, tortured, hopeless, has taken over my body and my mind. I am in the power of evil.

I wish they were not coming. I do not know how to summon anyone to meet them. There is no one here.

Harriet of course came in with them . . . I heard her whispering in the hall, "Miss Spencer has failed rapidly in the last weeks . . . be prepared for a change . . ." (This to Lisa, I presume.)

Lisa ran in and, much to my surprise, kissed me. "I am so glad to see you, and I've brought you Eva."

Poor dear Eva was clearly in a state of shock, and I

don't wonder. At first she was so overcome with shyness and not knowing what to say to the wreck before her, that she hardly looked at me. She sat in the chair by the bed, her hands clasped, and a look of fierce determination on her face to see the ordeal through. Lisa tactfully withdrew and closed the door behind her.

What did I say? Some casual remark about its being good of her to come, and good of Lisa to bring her.

"Oh, my dear Miss Spencer, you've been crying," she wailed. "It's a terrible place!" I had tried to imagine what it would be like to see her again, but it had never occurred to me that she would break down herself. She fumbled in her bag and drew out a box of candied ginger. The dear old thing had remembered that I love it.

"Let's have a piece right away. It'll cheer us up," I said.

But all I felt was an immense weariness before the effort of making contact across such an abyss of time and pain. We talked for about a half hour and by the end she was able to tell me a little about herself, the arthritis in her hands (they are quite warped and gnarled) and news of various acquaintances . . . but it is all so far away, I could only pretend interest. Harriet came in twice, officiously, to bring cups of coffee and coffee cake.

"She seems kind," Eva murmured, but with a look of bewilderment in her eyes. I suppose she sensed things she could not really get hold of. And there is no point in my even trying to tell anyone about torture. Too easy for that to be laid aside as senility, the paranoia one hears about. I don't know what I said in answer. The visit was simply a disaster. It is far too great an effort to try to pin down all the reasons. When Lisa came in, poor Eva was crying un-controllably, and hardly able to say goodbye.

Dear Lisa looked upset, too—I suppose I have changed since we had that good talk in the garden. She kissed me goodbye and whispered in my ear that she would send her father to see me.

I did not cry even after they had gone. I have become numb where human beings are concerned. I cannot af-ford to feel anything at all. I am walled in. I do not want to see anyone and shall have Richard turned away if he does come. The time for hope is past. Shall I ever have the strength for action? I have hidden the lighter fluid in the top drawer of the bureau under my scarves. Must find some way of getting two or three more cans.

When everything else has died, does violence still re-main? I am kept alive only for one purpose, to end things here while I am still sane enough to do it. But I must, to succeed, be clever, appear to be passive and weak. Ap-pear to be tamed, even grateful for small mercies. (The ginger, after so much flat-tasting food, is delicious.)

Now Eva has come and gone, I remember very dis-tinctly my little house, the porch hidden by vines, so it was very cool and green, the front parlor where I kept a wood fire burning all through the winter, and my books . . . oh, my books! The trouble is that the relationship Eva and I had was clear and simple, but it had to do with keeping the house shining clean. I guess there was just no substance we could fall back on here, no thread to pick up. At this season I was apt to be outdoors planting bulbs when she came. Then at noon we had a sandwich and tea together. And what on earth did we talk about? I cannot remember—the gossip of the town, I suppose, the cost of living. There is nothing left of all that. It's all gone.

Just now I looked out and it was snowing, the sky closed down, hard, relentless. I used to love the snow. Here it feels ominous. Even the weather slowly turns into the enemy—except, if we got snowed in, that would be the time for a cleansing holocaust!

I am full of panic these days. I wake sometimes with the hair clinging to my scalp, the sweat of panic. What am I so afraid of? I am afraid of Richard because he is so good he might manage to puncture my resolve to put a violent end to this place. I do not want to see anyone at all. Yet at the same time I wonder whether, if he does come, I should not give him the three copybooks I have filled, a kind of testament, should I be committed to the State Hospital, or in case I manage to carry out my plan. Perhaps if this story of despair could be published it would help those who deal with people like me, the sick in health or mind, or the just plain old and abandoned. I could not bear to have him read the last pages since X left but I believe he can be trusted not to, until I die. What will it matter then that I became infatuated with a woman and longed for her touch?

As I reread those words they make my spirit shrivel into itself. Have I allowed something real, something

pure, to be corrupted? Am I so unsure of myself that I
have come to believe what "they" say about me?

No, it is more that there is some truth in what they
think, yet, if people know nothing about love they will al-
ways make it into a sexual matter. The limit of what I
longed for with X was simply to lie down somewhere be-
side her and to hold her hand—Why that? Because words
were not a possible means of deep exchange between us,
because I longed so to rest in her, to believe too that she
might rest in me.

Now in late October I am able to listen to music again,
but not in the way I did before. It is a drug. I do not lis-
ten, just go on long wandering journeys and fantasies—
music is a door into escape now. I go over and over every
word Anna ever said to me. She said I was beautiful. And
that she had never known anyone like me. She used to
look at me with such a tender, amused look sometimes—is
that what women have most deeply to give to each other?
Tenderness? Oh, I should never have started on this
taboo subject.

The trouble is I have little else to feed on. Lately it has
been hard to concentrate. I read the paper and that's
about all. Everything I do is done to kill time. When I try
to read a book, my mind wanders—I find I have read the
same paragraph a dozen times.

The atmosphere has changed since Harriet came back,
changed for the worse. I mean *their* atmosphere. Rose is
in the doghouse, perhaps because she permitted Anna to
raise the standards. The old men are restless and peevish.
Several have refused to eat. Rain for several days. The

mud around the house is a morass. Only the geese are
cheerful and I hear they are afraid of foxes and huddle in
the doorway at night, poor creatures. Harriet talks about
getting rid of them. I am not asked into the kitchen for a
cup of tea or coffee anymore—not, perhaps, since the
inspectors came. I am not trusted. That is the frightful
joke on me. I, who can trust no one and who have been
betrayed, am the one who is *not trusted*. Everything here
is twisted around into reverse. I long only to manage to
burn the place down. But I am losing my grip, even the
grip on anger. Wouldn't it be wonderful if the house were
struck by lightning? An act of God!

Richard Thornhill has been here. He brought me five
novels and stayed quite a while. I learned by his visit that
I have changed for the worse. I simply did not have the
gumption to receive him as he deserves. I didn't want to
talk at all. I must have seemed churlish.

I could not bring myself to give him the copybooks. I
feel they should be in a safe place, my last will and testa-
ment. But if I let them go, and can no longer reread to
assure myself that I exist and have not dreamed all that
has happened here, I shall have lost my last hold on real-
ity. Today I could not remember Standish Flint's name!

The trouble was I could not tell Richard about Anna.
He asked me how things were going, but did not inquire
directly about her. I wanted so much to ask him to re-

mind Lisa that she had—how long ago?—said she would take me there for a visit. I am afraid of everything now. It would be an immense piece of courage to go and see Anna in her own home, for the very idea fills me with a tumult of emotion. So I am glad, in a way, that I was silent on this matter, as on so many others.

I cannot read the novels.

All I want is to sleep and to be left alone.

It must be mid-November. The leaves are all gone. Harriet found Pansy on my bed and now locks her out every night. The walls close in on every side. I do not remember things very clearly . . . is my brother John still alive? Where has Anna gone?

Soon it will be Thanksgiving. I used to help my mother stuff the turkey and make cranberry sauce her special way, so each cranberry shone like a jewel in a coat of sugar. The aunts came, though rarely Aunt Isabel. My father carved very skillfully and made little jokes, his jokes as much a part of the ritual as creamed onions and squash and mince pies. John and I thought dinner would never end—we had to stay till the nuts were cracked and a glass of port had been consumed by the adults. I can remember very well how hard the back of my chair felt and how we raced out into the chill fresh air, got on our bikes, and once rode way out into the country and got lost. Is John still alive, I wonder? Who but me remembers? It's all melting away . . . like snow . . . a whole lifetime . . . nothing.

The fact is that I am dying for lack of love. Exactly as though the oxygen in my lungs were being slowly diminished.

Mr. Coughlin, the diabetic, died yesterday. His nephew and niece came, of course. They, who had not bothered to see him more than once a month, if that, while he was alive, hurried over at once to arrange for the funeral. This time I notice that the vivid reaction among the old men when Standish died is not there. They seem hardly to have noticed when the body was removed. Strangely enough, Rose mourned him. She was weeping when she brought in my lunch.

"He is better off, Rose," I said gently. "He's hardly known where or who he was for months."

"It's just . . . just . . ." but she couldn't express what she felt and ended by saying quite angrily, "I hate this place!"

"You're not alone in that," I murmured. Probably she didn't hear me, and that is just as well. But I am interested in the violence of her feeling. I suppose she is caught just as we are. Being with the moribund day after day can't be easy on the psyche, and her way has been to be on the defensive against compassion. Compassion would cost too much, I suppose.

When I reread this journal or whatever it is, I am amazed at the vitality I had when I came here—about six months ago. My mind was alive. Now it is only alive in spots and at moments, maybe a half hour a day when something like Rose's unexpected tears wakes it. I no longer function as a human being. Even weeks ago I had ideas of taking action—violent action—of burning the place down. I still have the lighter fluid. It is like the little baskets of food or ornaments that were laid in the Egyptian tombs beside the mummy of a king or queen—a talisman.

The day after Thanksgiving—no, Saturday, I think.

Yesterday the walls of Jericho came down to Lisa's trumpet! She appeared out of the blue, looking full of surprises, bringing me an Advent wreath, so pretty, with candles on it. (My idea is to hide the candles for other purposes. They will be part of my arsenal of matches, lighter fluid and other combustibles.) But she came also to help me dress and to take me down to see Anna. It all happened so quickly I had no time to think or to say no. I put on my pink sweater and tweed skirt and my liberty scarf, and remembered to take the Hermès blouse, still wrapped in tissue paper after she had washed and ironed it for me when she was here.

Luckily Lisa talked a blue streak the whole way. She is

finding the freshman year very exciting, especially a
course in cultural anthropology. That and Russian are her
great enthusiasms. She poured it all out, and I listened
gratefully. It's been months since I've left the home—
everything we saw was vividly exciting—a black dog
barking as we went by, the lovely withered beech leaves,
pale brown against all the blacks and grays, a flock of
jays, a woodpecker, and once a startlingly blue pond, re-
flecting the cloudless sky.

Anna's farm is about five miles away, along a winding
road that follows a brook. I felt I was inside a painting, a
Brueghel perhaps. Children in bright red caps and stock-
ings. A man with a gun, out for deer. Why am I writing
all this down? I suppose to keep from remembering what
it was like to see Anna again.

The farm was just as I had imagined it, classic even to
geraniums in the windows, a huge red barn, and a big
vegetable garden in the field to one side, nothing but
pumpkins and withered stalks now. Anna came out be-
fore Lisa had even come to a halt. Anna herself. I have
dreamed this woman so deeply, then buried the dream so
deeply, I felt nothing at all. I felt encased in armor. It
was something to go through as well as possible, like
death.

"Dear Miss Spencer," she said, taking my hand warmly
in hers, and thanked Lisa for bringing me. "Come in." We
sat down a little self-consciously in the front parlor, only
Lisa at ease.

"I've been waiting for a letter . . ." Anna said with her

sweet, slightly teasing smile. "How come I never got one?" Of course she didn't know the horrible truth.

"I wrote, but I guess it never got to the post office."

"Oh my," Anna said miserably. "Do you think she'd do that?"

"It doesn't matter."

"I've thought about you every day, wondered. I called once and they said you were sick. But, you know, they don't welcome a call. I should have tried again. We've been that busy, first getting the hay in, then the vegetables. I've put up hundreds of jars, it feels like . . ."

Anna, usually so silent, was voluble. It came from shyness. I sat there, numb and dumb, wishing Lisa would have the sense to leave us alone. Then hordes of grandchildren came in to be introduced, and the husband, a tall dark man with a scowl who made his escape as fast as he decently could. But—saving grace!—he asked Lisa if she'd like to see the cows, and they all trooped out to the barn.

Then Anna and I sat, in the parlor, on stiff chairs, not daring to look at each other, while the immense silence flowed in, not the silence of companionship and understanding that we had known in the days at the farm, but the silence of psychic discomfort. A wall of silence between us. I could not speak, lit a cigarette, and Anna went out to fetch an ashtray. When she came back, I gave her the blouse.

"Oh, but you shouldn't, Miss Spencer—it's so becoming!"

"I want you to have it," I said firmly.

"Well," she had grown quite pink, "I'll think of you when I wear it. It's very kind of you."

For the first time she really looked at me. And I looked back.

"You don't look well, Miss Spencer. You look dragged out."

"I'm on the downgrade, Anna. Might as well face it."

"I wish I could take care of you!" For the first time she sounded like herself and I had to laugh, for the sheer relief of it.

"We haven't got much time." Suddenly anxious lest someone spoil this moment, I rushed in to try to say something. "I'm so glad I knew you for a little while. I wish I could tell you what it meant, what I tried to say in the letter . . ." Then I almost broke down and told her how they had killed my love, and I wish I had. But sitting there in the parlor it all seemed a little strange, too strange to utter. Perhaps I kept my self-respect and her respect by not saying it.

I didn't see anything all the way back, I was just hoping I could get back to my bed and turn my face to the wall and not weep in front of Lisa. Neither of us said very much. As soon as she had left, I ferreted out the tranquilizers—I suppose that is what they are—that they used to give me, and swallowed three. I slept the whole afternoon. I'm dead now, or might as well be. Something has gone, some spring, some fresh response to life I used to have. Is this old age? Not caring? I would not have believed that until now. I would have said that was a myth created by the young so as not to worry about the old. "They don't really care any more."

The tide goes out, little by little; the tide goes out and whatever is left of us lies like a beached ship, rotting on the shore among all the other detritus—empty crab shells, clam shells, dried seaweed, the indestructible plastic cup, a few old rags, pieces of driftwood. The tide of love goes out. Anna is now one with Alex and all the others, hardly distinguishable. I can say of them all, "I loved you once, long ago." And what is left of you? A lapis lazuli pin, a faded rose petal, once pink, slipped into the pages of this copybook.

But, ironically enough, I, Caro, am still here. I still have to manage to die, and whatever powers I have must be concentrated on doing it soon. I want my death to be something more like me than slow disintegration. "Do not go gentle into that good night" . . . the words, so hackneyed by now, come back to me like a command from somewhere way down inside, where there is still fire, if only the fire of anger and disgust.

I feel quite sure that Harriet puts tranquilizers in my coffee and that it is Sanka. Today I threw it down the john and asked for a second cup, "real coffee"—I went out into the kitchen and they couldn't very well hide anything there. I sat at the table, but they were at their antics again, and told me I had heard from John last week. I have no memory of this.

"Oh yes, Miss Spencer, I brought you a card from Florida."

(Of course they are spies as well. If there was such a card Harriet must have read it and thrown it away.)

They are very clever about confusing me and it's quite evident that they do it on purpose.

"Is it December?" I asked. Outside it is a grim, cold day with a high wind rattling the dead leaves.

"No, dear, it's November 28th. Thanksgiving was last week."

But how am I to believe the slightest thing? Even to the date? They are driving me slowly to the wall, driving me into senility, and for them that means complete passivity. When I am a vegetable they will be glad.

"Miss Spencer is more cheerful these days," Harriet said to Rose in that way she has as if I were not in the room. "She doesn't cry anymore, do you, dear?"

"I expect not."

"Do you remember how you used to cry?"

"No," I lied, and saw them exchange a look—mad as a hatter!

Later when I lay down and began to write, I realized for the flash of a second what this atmosphere does. They never tell me the truth and I pretend to believe their lies. Then I lie to them and little by little every shred of truth, of reality, is destroyed. I have stopped crying because I am dead inside.

Anyway, I won about the candles. Harriet came and took the wreath away, to hang in the front window, she told me.

"Didn't Miss Thornhill bring candles?"

"Maybe she forgot" I prevaricated.

"Hmmm," Harriet sniffed and went away.

I have hidden the candles under my underwear in a drawer but I've got to think of a better place. Under the mattress they might break. Maybe in my empty suitcase? No one would think of looking there. I am not about to go on a journey.

The best news is that Ned brings the trash cans in every night because a raccoon has been knocking them over and makes a fearful mess outside. Harriet is trying to cajole him into building a shed that could be padlocked. But so far he has shown no interest at all in performing this task.

"Why bother?" I heard him say. "It's no trouble to bring the cans in."

If I can set the trash cans on fire all will be well. Ned and Harriet sleep in a bedroom off the kitchen so they would hear any loud noise, but my guess is they sleep soundly, and the door is locked. Tonight I'll practice going out there, so I know just what I might run into. If they wake, I can pretend that I feel dizzy and sick and was looking for some Alka Seltzer.

I have to be sure that Pansy is not indoors. Thank goodness the old dog was put to sleep some time ago. He would have barked. I could put some lighter fluid on the curtains—a quick blaze.

I must also find out whether there is a fire extinguisher and see if I can manage to put it out of commission. I really feel awake and able to cope for the first time in weeks. The adrenal gland seems to be working again. And that cup of real coffee excited me.

I wonder what it's like to die in a fire? I guess you suffocate. It can't take very long.

But now I must be very careful. It has to be done in a blizzard when the fire engines either can't get up here or are slowed down. And how can I keep myself alert that long? December, January . . . the big snows don't come till January. And what if I lose my nerve? Right now I do not feel ready. Something is still to happen—I don't know what—before I can feel ready.

The only person I mind about is Jack . . . is there some way to get him out? Warn him? No, that would be too risky. The old men are better off dead. I have no compunction whatever about giving them a quick blazing end. It's more than they deserve, poor creatures.

My Aunt Isabel would fully approve of this criminal act. I can hear her saying, "Only cows go meekly to the slaughter. You're a brave woman, Caro. And you're not crazy enough to let them have it their way, to carry you out addled and totally gone to seed . . . no, Caro, you'll go out in a blaze!"

At present all this is still a fantasy, something to keep me going from day to day. And I repeat with ironic satisfaction Eliot's lines,

> We only live, only suspire
> Consumed by either fire or fire.

There is only one fire in me now, a fire of disgust and hatred, and there is plenty of fuel to keep it going till January in this place.

It is strange that now I have made my decision I can prepare for death in a wholly new way. I feel free, beyond attachment, beyond the human world at last. I rejoice as if I were newborn, seeing with wide-open eyes, as only the old can (for the newborn infant cannot see) the marvels of the world. These late November skies are extraordinary . . . great open washed-in color, a transparent greenish-blue, a wonderful elevating pink. The trees are so beautiful without their leaves. I lie on my bed and sometimes just look for hours in a daze of quiet pleasure.

I listen to music again. Last night the Mozart Adagio and Fugue for Strings in C Minor. It is years since I listened to it with Alex at a concert in London. Now I listened to it quite differently . . . the memory of passion added nothing. The music alone was with me. I felt exalted and purified.

I have believed since I came here that I was here to prepare for death, but I did not yet know how to do it. At first I felt I must cling to myself, keep my mind alive somehow—That was the task set before me, a losing battle, for the best I could hope for was to stand still in the same place. Progress in an intellectual sense was clearly out of the question. It ended in greater and greater frustration and anger.

I see, now that death is not a vague prospect but something I hold in my hand, that the very opposite is required from what I thought at first. I am asked to listen

to music, look at the bare trees divested of all but their
fine structure, drink in the sunset like wine, read poetry
again. I have laid novels aside. (The human world in the
sense of relationship is not mine to worry about or to par-
take of any longer. It is not my concern.) I am gathering
together all that matters most, tasting it for the last time.
As I do this, everything mundane falls away. Why, it
seems quite stupid that I have minded drinking coffee
from a plastic cup! How foolish can one be?

Harriet and Rose come and go through the room like
ghosts. They have no power to irritate or confuse. So for
the first time I am able to be kind to *them*. That is be-
cause they have lost their power to hurt.

And how has this immense change taken place? It
came from seeing Anna again and letting that whole bur-
den of love and shame fall away, all tension of that sort
gone from me . . . and it then came from making the de-
cision to end this whole business in a cleansing burst of
flame. I am knotted up to a single purpose now. What a
relief! I am stripped down to nothing, needing no protec-
tion anymore. All needs have been fulfilled. Is this mad-
ness, God?

I believe it is close to it. But perhaps at the furthest
reach and in the presence of death there is no distinction
to be made. Absolute nakedness may be madness. It
doesn't matter. It is what is *required*.

And when we have achieved it, then perhaps we are
able to give the ultimate things. At some earlier stage it
might have been love. Now it must be an end to misery
and corruption for the body, a clean quick end. We give

when we have nothing. Then there is no wall between us and the living or the dead. We are all one.

I look at the old men with a new tenderness, the curious way they revolve around Jack, the only youngish person in the house. There he sits rocking all day, always cheerful except very rarely when he gets angry . . . as who doesn't? The other night a fox must have been in the vicinity for the geese were restless, squawked in fear and huddled against the door. At about ten there was a real commotion and Jack called out in his strange strangled voice. I got out of bed to see what the matter was, opened the door, and whatever it was got frightened off. By then Harriet had arrived in her wrapper, bare feet, furious at being awakened.

"Jack was worried about the geese," I explained. "He thinks there may be a fox out there."

"And what if there is?" she screamed. "Can't I get a night's sleep for once? Who cares about the geese? Good riddance, I'd say."

At this rough speech, Jack suddenly howled and sobbed like a child. "P—p—poor geese," he stammered, "Jack doesn't w—w—ant them to die!"

"Now, Jack," she said more gently, "they'll be all right. I'll send Ned out with his rifle. Go to bed, Miss Spencer, you'll catch cold. All we need is an epidemic of colds around here."

I fled, fearing worse. But none of us slept the rest of the night. Mr. Thompson had a nightmare and gave a muffled scream. Fred Smith, who so rarely speaks, went off on a jag of some kind, some childhood memory about a goose. "He was a holy terror," he kept saying, "goosed the schoolteacher one day." Then he giggled and nearly choked to death. "Chased old Mr. Brown half a mile down the road," and he gave a whoop. Jack repeated the phrase and laughed and laughed. That room of old men had become a nursery in the middle of the night. I was dying to get up and make them cups of cocoa, but I didn't dare.

And now I have just heard that Harriet plans to have the geese killed and put in the freezer. It will be a relief as I have been anxious about them. They should not have been left with no shelter these cold nights. I myself feel the draft from the window, a thin stream of icy air. It gives me neuralgia. Tried to stuff Kleenex along the sills, but Harriet tore it all out.

"I'm cold in the night," I explained.

"Nonsense, you have two blankets. Pull one up over your head."

And still I wait for whatever it is that has to happen. Some outrage or cataclysm, some galvanizing event that will give me the courage to act.

It's December, they tell me. I have stopped reading the newspaper. Marooned. The trouble is that now I have come right up to the inexorable FACT: I have to admit that I do not want to die. Soon it will snow. Soon I will have to be ready. But I am not. I feel terribly restless and

have taken to pacing about, a thing that irritates Harriet
and Rose—I always seem to be in their way when they
pass with a bedpan or broom. But how does one fill time
waiting . . . waiting .

I have to admit that in some ways I am treated with
kindness these days. Harriet washed my hair yesterday,
maybe to try to tire me out! Tomorrow Richard Thornhill
is to pay a visit. I really have no wish to see him . . . I
have to conceal so much. Can't tell him my plans, of
course. Might pretend madness . . . and should I give
him the early copybooks? I cannot bear to part with
them. Yet how to save them when the time comes? I am
all at sixes and sevens, pacing around in limbo.

"We have to get you out of here," was what Richard
came to say. Why was my reaction so violent? Even a
month ago such words would have been a reprieve, but I
burst into tears and begged him not to do anything, not
to take me away. "I have to die here," I said. "It's too late
. . . too late!"

He took my hand and held it then and calmed me
down.

"No one is going to force you, dear Miss Spencer."

"Having one of her spells, is she?" Harriet came in with
warm milk. I held the cup in my two hands like a baby.

Then Richard closed the door.

I lay on my bed as heavy as a corpse. A very strange

sensation. I had my eyes closed. I didn't care whether he stayed or not. But he did stay, silent there beside me for a while. Then he talked about other things—how much Lisa is looking forward to seeing me when she comes home in two weeks for a weekend. Her young man has decided to go back to college and become a doctor after all. While Richard talked I managed very slowly to come back to the surface. At last I could open my eyes.

He reached over again and took my hand. His felt so warm and comforting, I looked deeply into his eyes for a second.

"I am stripped down to nothing," I said. "So somehow I can see you very clearly, and everything else. I want you to know that whatever happens you did all that you could. You have been a good friend."

"We are all wound round in mystery," was his answer.

It was as though we were the last people left alive on earth. I do not really know what happened, why it was like that. I felt I was speaking to someone very far away, yet someone who would hear a whisper, and perhaps I did whisper,

"Can you forgive me now?"

The strange thing, the marvel was that he did not say what at any other time he might have said, something about my not needing to be forgiven. He understood that I was in extremity and he did not question it.

"I believe we are forgiven at the instant of asking forgiveness, for asking forgiveness is an act of faith. It places the soul in eternity."

"But I am thinking of terrible things, Richard. Do you believe in damnation?"

"I don't know. Do you?"

"Yes. But I think I am going to risk it . . . when the snow falls."

Then there was a long silence.

The man was clearly suffering with me and for me. His silence was so intense I felt almost as though he was a laser beam, probing, probing, trying to reach to the very marrow of my thought. I saw the sweat on his forehead. It was all very strange.

Then something snapped. Like people who have been dreaming, we woke.

Richard coughed. We were back in the normal world. I noticed a spider web in the corner of the room, and the way a band of sunlight lay across the floor. I looked around me.

"You are a great person, Miss Spencer."

"I wish you could bring yourself to call me Caro."

"I think of you as Miss Spencer. It is a sign of respect. I don't come across so very many great human beings."

I had to smile at that. It seemed so nonsensical.

"No, I mean it. Don't smile. I have seen in you what courage can be when there is no hope. I have seen the power of a human being to withstand the very worst and not be corrupted, and not change."

"I have changed."

"Not in any way that affects the essence. You are beautiful."

He must have gone then, or someone knocked on the door. I can't quite remember now. I remember that I felt terribly tired and perhaps I slept.

"Well, thank goodness, you've come to!" I head Harriet's voice, "you've been lying there like a corpse. Your pulse was so low I could hardly catch it. What *have* you been doing?"

I was given a drink, a thimbleful of brandy.

I felt shivery and queer and decided to have a hot bath before supper and get into bed. When I was in the bathroom running the water, I realized that in my confused state I had forgotten my soap and face cloth. I was barefooted and must have made no sound at all, for when I came to my room Harriet was sitting on the bed reading the last copybook. I had left it open there with the pen inside it. She looked extremely startled to see me, and for just a second we stared at each other. Then I felt such a flood of fierce strength rise in me that I must have lunged at her like a wild animal, torn the copybook out of her hands and in doing so knocked her off balance so she fell to the floor.

"Rose! Help!" She screamed, but she was not hurt, only

panting with anger and the effort of lifting her two hundred pounds up. I met Rose in the corridor as I ran to the bathroom, still clutching the copybook, and locked myself in.

Harriet stood outside shouting at me, "I know your evil thoughts, cursing us! Attacking me! That's assault and it's a federal offense in case you're interested!"

"Come on, Harriet," I heard Ned say. "She's crazy, poor thing . . . leave her be!"

"She'll go without supper, that's for sure."

I could have laughed at the impotence of this punishment. What do I care about supper?

I have been here now for a long time. Maybe hours. Everything is as I dreamed it would be. It is snowing hard. I can peer out of the bathroom window at whiteness, a fur of whiteness against the panes. All I have to do now is wait for them to go to bed. I wish I had my watch on, but I took it off when I undressed. But I can tell by the sounds, and eventually by the silence. And meanwhile I am going to lie down on the bathmat with my back against the door and have a little nap. I feel at peace. Death by fire will come as an angel, or it will come as a devil, depending on our deserts.

Only one thing, THE important thing I must manage to do is place all the copybooks in the frigidaire. To you who may one day read this, I give them as a testament. Please try to understand.

AFTERWORD

This manuscript was found after the fire that destroyed the Twin Elms Nursing Home. In a letter found inside the cover, Miss Caroline Spencer requested the Reverend Thornhill to have it published if possible. This has been done with the permission of her brother, John Spencer.